Ernie Pyle

ERNIE PYLE IN ENGLAND

Ernie Pyle in England
(1941)

CONTENTS

ERNIE PYLE IN ENGLAND

For
That Girl
Who Waited

FOREWORD

Last fall when the great air battles were being fought out over England and the first full reality of the bombed torment that was London's came over the cables to us in America, there grew in me an almost overpowering urge to be there amidst it all. To this day I cannot quite put into words just what my feelings were. I am a professional traveler, but it was not curiosity "to see what it was like" that made me want to go. And I am a newspaperman, yet the "story" I might send back hardly entered my mind at all. I simply wanted to go privately — just inside myself I wanted to go.

For it seemed to me that in London there was occurring a spiritual holocaust — a trial of souls — that never again in our day could be reenacted. I felt that to live your span in this time of ours, and to detour around an opportunity of sharing in the most momentous happening of that time, was simply to be disinterested in living. It seemed to me somehow that anyone who went through the immersion into fear and horror of the London bombings, could not help but be made fuller by it.

So I went. Things didn't turn out just as I had expected. For one thing, it never seemed dramatic to me when I was there. All the elements I had visioned were there, yet apparently I had not the capacity for being erupted by them up into a great new nobleness of mind and heart. What I mean is that, so far as I can analyze myself, I feel no different than before I went. I don't feel cleansed in spirit or exalted in stature. I merely toasted my shins awhile before the grate of war; they — the people of England — are the embers and coals and licks of flame that constitute the very fire itself. We who go and come away again cannot be other than small beside them.

From the day war was declared, I felt keenly for the side of Britain. But I am no intellectual curator of the world's morals; the thinkers who take up the war as a "cause" leave me bewildered. I simply wanted England to win because it seemed to me safer and sounder for England to be running the world than for Germany to run it. And now that I've been there, I still feel exactly the same about it.

Somehow it seems inevitable that there shall be one dominant nation in the world. I guess it's just the same principle that makes Ivory Soap float, or that makes one horse, instead of all the entrants, win a race. Whichever nation is dominant sets the tempo for a good part of the world. And if the tempo-setter must be either England or Germany, it seems to me simple sanity that England should continue to be that nation.

The actual policy of a world rule is formed not so much by the leaders and individual representatives of a country as by the background of basic character of the whole people. And if I had never known it before, I discovered this winter that the national character of the British is a noble character. Sure, there are things about them we despise; there are intolerable Englishmen by the scores of thousands. Yet if you judge them by their massed heart and their massed way of dealing with life — which you must do if you're deciding who is to dominate the rest of the world — then the English seem to me to come off as leaders more nearly perfect than any other nation on earth.

I have almost no feeling at all against the Germans. I never did, and I still don't today, even after they had filled the sky with bombs above my own private and precious head. I don't see how anyone can blame Germany for wanting to be Mr. Big in this world. Doesn't England want to be Mr. Big too? And does America want to play second fiddle to Italy or Germany or Japan? Of course not.

You cannot help but be anguished at death and destruction, and sometimes you sink into a despair of abysmal hopelessness when you stand in the center of a complete ravage — and yet it's war and I can't blame Germany for fighting nor England for fighting back. They're both in there punching, and may the best man win. And if England isn't the best man, may she win anyhow, dammit.

As for my own case history, in the event you care, I'm a farmer who has forgotten how to farm, and a newspaperman of so many years' tenure that I no longer know how to do anything else on earth but work on and write for newspapers. I can't even sew on a button anymore.

It has been eighteen years since I quit school and went to work on a small Indiana daily, and every minute of that time has been spent on newspapers. I've run the gamut, as they say. I've worked every job on a newspaper from cub reporter to managing editor.

Nearly all of those eighteen years have been with the Scripps-Howard Newspapers. I doubt there has ever been a happier association with a business institution than mine. I've never had a boss who wasn't a gentleman; never had a superior who wasn't also my friend. Scripps-Howard has always been good to me, and liberal too. It was a nutty idea when I began pestering them, some six years ago, to let me cut loose from the desk and start wandering around in my car, writing a daily column about anything that popped into my head.

But they said okay, go ahead and try it. Since then I've covered 200,000 miles and been on five of the six continents and crossed both oceans and delved into every country in the Western Hemisphere and written upward of 1,500,000 words in that daily column.

It has been a joyous life. I've gone down the Yukon River on a stem-wheeler, and lived with the lepers in Hawaii, and petted llamas in the high Andes, and reveled in the strange lazy beauties of Rio. There isn't a state of the Union we haven't been in at least three different times.

By "we" I mean the other half of this gypsy combination, who is known to the readers of the column as "That Girl." Almost everywhere I have been, she has been too. She uses up her time by reading books and working Double-Crostix puzzles and absorbing knowledge and keeping me from jumping out of my skin. In all our little triumphs and all our big despairs, she has been along.

And then came England. That was different. The government wouldn't let her go. Her's was the far greater task of staying and waiting. But now the "Great Experience" is over, and we have hit the trail together again, in the old fashion, just wandering around talking to people and writing about the rain and things. At least I think we have. But maybe we're only fooling ourselves. Maybe we're just pretending that we've picked up the world where we left it last fall. For there is probably something to the theory that our lives, in common with all others, can never again be just as they were before 1940.

Ernie Pyle,
Los Angeles,
July, 1941.

PART I: ON MY WAY

1. QUALMS

New York,
November, 1940.

A small voice came in the night and said, "Go."
And when I put it up to the boss he leaned back in his chair and said, "Go."
And when I sat alone with my so-called conscience and asked it what to do, it pointed and said, "Go."
So I'm on my way to London.
Never before have I set out on a long trip with anything but elation in my heart. It is not so with this trip. This one is no lark. It will be tough and I know it.
I will be scared. I know I will feel small and in the way among a people who are doing a job of life and death.

2. CROSSING

Aboard S.S. Exeter,
December, 1940.

The sailing of a ship, the world over, is a gay event. A ship carries people out of reality, into illusion. People who go away on ships are going away to better things. But that was not true as we sailed for Europe. There was no gayety on the Exeter. Never, on any ocean or in any climate, have I seen a ship sail so drearily. I doubt there is a single person on board who goes joyously. Certainly no one is going for the fun of it. The Exeter takes its human cargo into the land of heavy reality, rather than from it. There were no farewell parties aboard ship. What few people had visitors to see them off sat in the lounges in small, quiet groups, talking seriously.

That Girl came to the ship with me. And so did an old friend we hadn't seen for years — Jim Moran, the fellow who hunted the needle in the public haystack, and who sold an icebox to an Eskimo. Maybe you've read about him. We knew Moran back when he was just an amateur crazy-man. He was a gay fellow to have around this day, and we were grateful for him. He tried his best to add a touch of joviality to the long-faced atmosphere of departure.

"Look at these passengers," Moran said. "Spies all over the place. Secret Agent Y-32. There goes Mata Hari of 1940. Everybody trying to eavesdrop on everybody else.

"Ernie, you need a dispatch case. Get an important-looking dispatch case and stuff it full of newspapers. Put a big padlock on it. Carry it everywhere with you. Carry it to meals. Walk the deck with it. Never put it down. Then, about four days out, walk away from your deck chair and leave it lying there. I'll bet half the people on board would get maimed in the rush to grab it"

And I said, "Oh Moran, shut up."

We were to sail at 11 a.m. But the word passed around that we wouldn't get away till several hours later. The uncomfortable quiet of anticlimax went over the ship.

Moran sat down and wrote four postcards for me to mail in Lisbon, so his friends would think he was over there.

They left the ship at noon — Moran and That Girl. We couldn't sit there any longer, just waiting for the last moment to come. I walked out into the pier shed with them. She slipped me a note she had written, and I put it in my pocket. We have known each other a long time.

We didn't try to say anything but just good-bye. And we made it quick. For a minute I watched them walking away, down the long pier shed. Then I went to my cabin and shut the door.

Finally, at two o'clock, we sailed. Everybody had gone. The dock was empty and dead. There was no shouting, no confetti, not even a handkerchief waved. The lonely dock simply drew away. Nothing more, as we sailed on a cold gray afternoon in November toward the darkness of Europe.

We have just thirty-one passengers aboard. That is only a quarter of the ship's normal capacity, and only a sixth of what it carries on the return trips. Coming back, they put cots in the lounge and pack in 180 or 190 people. But there are so few of us that everybody has a cabin to himself. Mine is a big one with two beds, a sofa-couch, a private bathroom and two portholes. Furthermore, it has a sunny veranda just outside the door. It is, I believe, the most comfortable cabin I've ever had aboard ship. All I need to set up housekeeping is a base-burner and a side of bacon.

We weren't two hours out of New York when we had boat drill.

There wasn't any monkey business about it, either. They swung out the boats, and tested the radio in No. 1 boat.

I figured that, due to the instability of world conditions (as some people call it), we would have boat drill every day. But there wasn't another until the seventh day out, when the whistle blew and the bells rang at eleven o'clock in the morning.

It turned into quite an experience for a British girl on board. She had just got up, and was taking a shower. When she heard the bells it never occurred to her that it might be a drill. She said to herself, "My God, this is it!" So she jumped out of the shower and into slacks and sweater without even drying. The lifebelts are on racks under the beds, and she got her lifebelt stuck and practically had to tear the bed down to get it out. She couldn't find her money, so she ran off without it. She tarried not for lipstick nor rouge. She arrived on deck pale and breathless — to find that we were only playing.

We are now getting into waters where ships do get sunk occasionally. But there is no anxiety on board about our safety. We are fully lighted at night, and on each side of the ship is painted a big American flag, with a spotlight rigged to shine on it. Every night I've been meaning to lay out my heavy clothes on the other bed and have everything all ready to jump into — just in case. But we're almost there now, and I haven't got around to it.

Some of the passengers have been hoping something exciting would happen. One favors picking up a couple of lifeboats from a sunken ship. Another wants a raider to stop us and search. One extremist even favors being fired at mistakenly by a submarine — on condition that the torpedo misses. As for me, I don't want to see anything in this ocean but waves. And on second thought I don't even want to see waves. For I'm seeing them right now; and to put it bluntly, they make me sick.

The run to Lisbon is tough these days for the dining room and cabin stewards. Going over, there are so few people their tips don't amount to much. And coming back, although the ship is loaded to the hilt, everybody is broke, so the tips are still small. But the crew does get a war bonus of $1 a day for working this run.

We have one Englishman aboard who is the most satisfactory listener I've ever talked with. He considers everything you say the most fascinating thing he's ever heard, and says so with a repertoire of ejaculations completely new to me.

For instance, you say you've been at sea a month this year, and he almost jumps out of his chair and says, "No! How extraordinarily remarkable!" You say something else, and he says, "God save us! Would you believe it?" You remark that planes are landing completely blind by radio beam these days, and he leans forward as if about to leap, and comes out with: "God's teeth! You don't say it!"

That last one is worth the whole voyage to me.

3. WAY STATION

Lisbon,
December, 1940.

You must call it "Leeze-bone," this only free seaport city left in Europe. If you say "Leeze-bone," then you're a bona-fide European traveler. If you say "Leeze-bo-ah" you're a Portuguese and live here. If you say "Liz-bun" you're a plain American.

Today Lisbon is the temporary pasture for all those of Europe fortunate enough to escape. It is the needle's eye through which must pass all non-fighting travel between Europe and anywhere else. A month ago it was estimated there were 20,000 refugees in Portugal. There are probably fewer now, for they are being worked out gradually, and Portugal has tightened her borders against newcomers. You can't get a visa for Portugal today unless you can show a ticket to take you on beyond.

Most of the refugees are in or around Lisbon. A good portion of them hope some day to get to North America. Others go to South America and the Belgian Congo; and since our arrival a whole shipload of Greeks has left for the Dutch East Indies. The majority of the refugees had money originally, or they couldn't have greased their flight from their home countries. But most of them couldn't bring much with them. And living costs in Lisbon, although low by our standards, are high by European standards. So the refugees live close to their belts. Lisbon is not a gay place of high night life.

The staff of the American consulate has been greatly enlarged, yet they are working as intensely as newspapermen just before edition time. All day long thick groups of people shove and push and wave papers before the consulate counters, trying to be next in line to argue for a visa for that haven of havens — America. Desperation drives people to many ruses. The consulate clerks have heard so many phony stories that they practically suspect everybody. Yet they seem to have an attitude of tender- ness toward them all, too, as if to say "You poor devils!"

Most of the refugees are German Jews and people from the Balkan countries. But now there are a large number of Belgians and French too. Many of them are trying to get to England. And England will take them in, if they can get there.

Restaurants in Lisbon are excellent. There are half a dozen that would satisfy any international epicure. Last night I had the best steak since Buenos Aires, and with all the trimmings it came to only eighty cents. Food abounds here; they pile it on, they even waste it — while the rest of Europe draws closer to starvation.

This is a hilly city — a beautifully hilly city. There are streets here nearly as steep as those in San Francisco. It is very white, and from a distance it glistens. And it is vastly larger than I had expected — nearly a million people —and there are traffic jams just as at home.

The sidewalks are made of flat-topped stones, walnut size, laid in weird designs of black and white as are the sidewalks in Rio. The streets are practically all of cobblestone. The city is dotted with parks and circles and statues.

There are some palm trees, and the other trees still have their leaves on them. But don't let such greenery, and such bright sun, and such blue skies, pull any wool over your eyes. A friend's description of southern California fits Lisbon perfectly right now. He said, "You can lie down under a rosebush in full bloom and freeze to death." That's Lisbon too, in December.

Three great warring nations all run regular passenger air lines into Lisbon. You can see planes take off every day for Berlin and Rome; and several times a week for England and the U. S. The downtown ticket offices of the English and German lines are next door to each other. In fact, I got into the German office by mistake, and naively asked about planes to London. The young man behind the counter directed me, in excellent English, to the British Overseas offices next door.

Theoretically, the air line to England is a commercial line. But the British Air Attaché here tells them whom to take, and when. When you arrive from the United States, England-bound, you register in a book at the ticket office of British Overseas Airways. That's all there is for you to do. That's all you can do. Some afternoon maybe a week later, maybe two months later, the ticket office will call up and tell you to get ready.

Passengers are chosen in the order of their "priority." Nobody goes without priority. This is arranged in London only, and the average traveler can't get priority at all. Being a newspaperman, I have priority. If I didn't have, I might as well go home. But when it will get me to London is anybody's guess. All you can do is wait.

What applies to us, applies to thousands here awaiting transportation. Trains are crowded. The Rome plane is booked three weeks ahead. Time is heavy on people's hands, and as the weeks drag on they draw their financial belts closer and closer. But at cocktail hour the bars are crowded, and you hear a dozen different tongues. Americans mostly gather at the Avenida, and give each other the day's developments — if any — in their struggle to get wherever they're going.

Even transportation to America is difficult. They say three hundred people are sitting here waiting for the Clipper. Seats on the Clipper have been "scalped" for $1000 — and then the buyer finds he has bought nothing, for Panair doesn't permit transfer of reservations. The American Export Line runs a weekly steamer to the United States, and it is booked two months ahead. But many of these bookings are for people who haven't even arrived from their home countries yet. Hundreds who have made reservations will never get their papers to go. They say that when the weekly boat sails, carrying out about two hundred people, it pretty well clears out those who are free to leave.

As far as I can tell, sentiment in Portugal is overwhelmingly pro-British. Some friends say they sense a lot of feeling for Germany here, but it doesn't seem that way to me. True, you see an occasional German army uniform on the streets. And you hear a good many people speaking German. But there is no way to tell whether these latter are fifth columnists or refugees.

Along with George Lait of the International News Service, who was a fellow passenger on the Exeter, I put up for several days at a pension, which is something half-way between a boarding house and a hotel. And from my slight experience with pensions in this and other countries, you can have them, and welcome. But by pulling wires, the two of us finally got a room in a hotel.

The new room is about twenty feet square, and it has two big windows that look onto a narrow street. Early each morning they bring all the newsboys and street vendors of Lisbon up to this street and test their lungs. If they can't wake us up, then they are weak and sick and are sent home for the day with a black mark.

Our room is old-fashioned, yet quite comfortable (except for temperature). The ceiling is far, far above us, and is covered with colossal scrollwork in purple plaster. The bathroom is simply one corner of the room walled off by movable panels, which stop five feet short of the ceiling. Our bathtub has three faucets, one marked cold, and two marked hot. The point is that one is a little hotter than the other. I don't know why it's done this way. All I care about is that one or the other should give off hot water; and they really do — plenty hot. But our radiator does not have the same virtue. It is a centuries old custom not to have heat over here. All radiators are vaguely warm; none is ever hot. They have no effect at all on the room's temperature.

I've been cold all over the world. I've suffered agonies of cold in Alaska and Peru and Georgia and Maine. But I've never been colder than right here in this room. Actually, the temperature isn't down to freezing. And it's beautiful outside. Yet the chill eats into you and through you. You put on sweaters until you haven't any more — and you get no warmer.

The result is that Lait and I take turns in the bathtub, I'll bet we're the two most thoroughly washed caballeros in Portugal. We take at least four hot baths a day. And during the afternoon, when I'm trying to write, I have to let the hot water run over my hands about every fifteen minutes to limber them up. I'm telling the truth.

We went down to see the Exeter sail. You'd never have recognized it as the placid and sparsely populated ship we came over on. In the lounge stood row after row of cots. Two-by-fours, with holes bored in them, had been laid over the rugs. The cot legs were set in these holes, to keep them from sliding in rough weather. Down below, every cabin was jammed. Cabins with three beds had four people in them. The ship was alive with children. Luggage was stacked everywhere.

The stewards were about to go completely crazy. Everybody was wanting something. And nobody could understand anybody. Bernie Garland, my steward coming over, said he could recognize about every language in Europe but he had a cabinful speaking something he'd never heard before.

On these homebound trips you're lucky to be aboard at all. Which made the request of one haughty woman sound ridiculous. I overheard it myself. She was in one of the best cabins, but she didn't like it. She came to the steward and asked if she was in first class. He told her there was only one class. So she said, "Well, you must have better cabins. Change my cabin right away, even if I pay more for it." She wanted to change — and with eighty people sleeping in public on cots!

PART II: ALL QUIET

1. PEACE TO WAR — SEVEN HOURS

England
December, 1940.

The phone rang in our hotel room in Lisbon, and we were told to be at the marine airport before daylight this morning. Don't think I didn't get all a-twitter. Our almost two solid weeks of waiting were drawing to an end, and Lait and I decided not even to go to bed.

Each of us left a small suitcase in Lisbon, to cut down the weight I put my excess necessities in a white sugar sack which a boat steward had given me. And so today I arrived in England carrying a small yellow bag, a typewriter, and a knotted-up sugar sack over my shoulder.

It was cold and eerie in the dimly lighted airport building at Lisbon. We walked up and down to keep warm, until finally the captain said, "Let's go." We followed the crew along a pier, and got into a motorboat. We could make out dimly the shapes of two big flying boats at anchor. As our boat eased up to one of them, we jumped through the door.

The plane had four motors, and was bigger than the Baby Clippers of Pan American Airways, but not as big as the regular Clippers. She was camouflaged.

The cabin was partitioned into three compartments, with smoking permitted in the rear one. I had supposed that these planes were stripped of all peacetime travel comforts to save weight, but not so. The seats were deep and comfortable, the floor was carpeted.

The steward gave us blankets. The engines were started, the door closed, and we taxied far out into the river. We could see the lights of the city on each shore. Suddenly the motors roared, and spray blinded the windows. We ran for what seemed a long time, surging through the water, until finally we felt her break free. The windows cleared and the shore lights dropped farther and farther below. The hot exhaust rings of the motors shone dramatically red in the darkness. We were on the way to England.

It might have been a flight in peacetime. Every one on the plane immediately went to sleep. I slept for a while, but curiosity got the better of me, and from daylight on I stayed awake.

Dawn found us over the ocean, with no land in sight. I had been told the flight would take ten hours, but we picked up a howling tailwind and came through in less than seven hours. Time didn't drag at all. Five hours out, I went through the plane and every passenger was asleep. As far as I could observe, not one person ever spoke to another during the trip. There were seven Americans aboard, one Swiss, and three Englishmen.

The steward served coffee and sandwiches, and later fruit. Then he came around and blacked out the windows so the passengers couldn't see out. This was done by putting a section of frosted glass over the regular windows, with rubber suction cups. This lets in light but prevents you from seeing out. I presume it is done to keep passengers from seeing convoys in the water below. But the joke was that the steward blacked out every window except mine. Either he ran out of frosted panes or else he thought I was blind. At any rate I stared out the window the whole trip.

Land came into view on the left. It was dark brown and bare, a high, rugged coast. I thought it was Ireland. We flew along this coast for an hour. The air got rough, and five passengers were very sick. Somehow I escaped that. We passed only two ships, both small. One of them flashed a signal to us with a blinker. We did not see a single plane on the trip.

Suddenly the pilot throttled down his motors and we started losing altitude. Then I realized we had not been flying along Ireland, but along the coast of England itself. We landed far out from shore among a lot of boats at anchor and camouflaged planes resting on the water. As we struck the surface there was that familiar long ripping sound.

I felt like a character in a dream. The journey from America was over. We had arrived. But it didn't seem really true. Any moment I expected to wake up and find myself still between those perpetual walls of the Hotel Europa in Lisbon.

A score of British officials, in raincoats and boots, came out in a motorboat and looked everything over, and a doctor took up the forms we had filled out. Then we all got into the boat. The men chatted with us all the way to shore. They said they would try to get us through the inspection in time to catch the mid-afternoon train to London, but they couldn't promise.

It was raining. We walked a hundred yards along the docks, then into the main street of the little town. There were soldiers on the street, carrying tin hats and gas masks. There were women in khaki uniforms, and many people on bicycles. All the store windows were crisscrossed with strips of paper. This tends to prevent shattering from the concussion when bombs explode in the neighborhood. Strips of many colors, pasted in many designs, made the town look as though it had been decorated for Christmas instead of patched up for the war.

I wish you could see that village street. It was like a picture from a Dickens novel. The gabled buildings, the language of the signs, the many smoking chimney pots were all the England of fiction, so peaceful, neat and secure. I had not been ashore three minutes before I was in love with England.

We were escorted to a big ground-floor room, the temporary office of the British Overseas Airways. There were easy chairs and couches and a coal fire in the grate, and a boy was serving hot tea. It took us two hours to get through all the inspections. We were taken one at a time into a room where two men questioned us. They asked about our purpose in coming, about our money, about whom we knew, and so on. It was by no means a grilling. They did it in a way that made you feel you were just sitting there chatting. The procedure was more than courteous; it seemed genuinely friendly.

After that they went through our baggage minutely. They even read our letters. But so great is English courtesy that the customs man asked me to take each letter from its envelope for him. He evidently thought it would be prying for him to do so! And then as train time drew near he said we would have to hurry to catch it, so he closed the bags without finishing the inspection, gave us advice about trains and the blackout in London, and hustled us into a waiting car provided by the air line.

We drove for fifteen minutes through a thickly settled suburb. They told us bombs had fallen in the street a few afternoons ago, but we saw no evidence of it. The suburb was like a continuation of the main street of that first town — neat as a pin, snug, comfortable and beautiful.

The train came right on schedule. The porter, an old man, stowed our bags away carefully and told us just when we would get to London. It would be after dark, he said, and the Germans would probably be overhead, but he said for us not to worry.

My very first impression of England was of lovely, courteous people. And I don't mean to us visitors so much as to each other. It is true that they are especially nice to Americans right now, but I noticed that they were just as thoughtful among themselves.

My only contact with English people before had been in the colonies. I had assumed that the ordinary Englishman had the same personality as those in far-off lands who gather in the clubs and hotels of an afternoon for their gin and tonic and who consider themselves superior to anything else on land or sea. But the Englishman in mass, at home, bears no resemblance at all to that. He always seems to have a pleasant little remark to make. He is interested instead of blas6. He is considerate, and he seems to enjoy being alive.

An English friend of mine says all this is true. But he says further that it is truer now than ever before. He says the war has done a lot for English character. He says it has drawn the people together, made them prouder of each other, made them humbler, and hence both mellower and stronger.

Anyway, I know that in all my traveling I have never visited a new country that in a few short hours filled me with the warmth that I feel for England.

2. "HE HASN'T COME YET, SIR."

London,
December, 1940.

We rode in luxury on our way to London town. We rode in a private compartment. We smoked, and read London newspapers, and drank tea, and ate ham sandwiches. We traveled through a magnificently green countryside. The fields looked more like parks than farms. It seemed odd that everything should be so green in December. It was a beautiful afternoon, not too cold. It would rain a little while, then the sun would come out bright.

Our first three hours in England had been so pleasant, the country so serene, the tea so true to tradition, it didn't seem possible that death and destruction could lie only three hours ahead. But it lay nearer than that.

We were drinking tea when Lait said "Look!" and there in the sky ahead silver barrage balloons were floating. There weren't just a few, but scores, even hundreds. They stretched on for miles and miles. We knew their presence indicated we were coming to a good-sized city.

And then came the first sight of destruction. I don't remember specifically what was the first bombed thing we saw, for we had barely seen the first when we saw a second and a third. Then wreckage became constant. I remember a crater in a suburban street, then wrecked houses near by, and a small factory burned. After that, for block after block, half the buildings we saw were wrecked. Some of the suburban stations where the train stopped were shattered, but people by the hundreds got off and on.

If I were to say there were strain and worry and fear on people's faces I certainly would be overworking my imagination. Except for the ghastly scenery, life seemed thoroughly normal.

An old man got into our compartment and sat down. He was ragged and feeble, and until he spoke I couldn't have told him from an eighty-year-old Missouri farmer. When the conductor looked in for the tickets he said to the old man, "Sorry, but you have to move back. You've got a third-class ticket, and here you are in first." The old man, in an accent that would be British wherever the sun sets, said, "Oh dear, oh dear" feebly, and took himself up and out. We wished he could have stayed.

Back home I had seen newsreel pictures of bombed buildings, but somehow I thought the real thing would look different. It doesn't. The only thing different is that now it's real and you feel a revulsion and a small sinking feeling with the knowledge of the awful power of a single bomb. You feel what it could do to you personally.

Finally we left the city and its wreckage behind and were out in green country again. Every open field had something in it to keep enemy planes from landing. Some fields were crisscrossed with row after row of tall white poles. Others had rolls of wire. Some had shallow ditches. Some had mounds of earth piled up in rows so geometrically regular that you would have thought they were planting crops instead of building obstructions.

Occasionally you would get a glimpse of a silver balloon pulled down into a woods to nestle until nightfall. Twice we passed antiaircraft guns out in the fields under canvas canopies, painted so like shrubbery that we could hardly identify them.

Every tree, every field, every cricket ground, every house and street seemed to be doing its bit. In the backyards of suburban homes along the railroad tracks there were somber marks of what war has done to the English way of life. I mean private bomb shelters; almost every backyard had one.

From the train window a shelter looked like just a large mound of dirt. From closer up, it could be seen to be a half-underground cellar, walled with concrete and sheet metal and covered heavily with dirt, much like the outdoor cellars of our Western prairies. We were interested to see vegetables growing on the earthen tops of many shelters.

All this, you must remember, was still a long way from London.

Now dusk came on, and we could no longer see fields nor bomb shelters. The conductor came through and asked us to black out the compartment. The windows have black shades on rollers, which you pull down and hook at the bottom. The windows themselves are painted black except for a square in the middle, and this is fully covered when you pull the curtain. A faint blue light shines at the top of the compartment

Thus we rode on toward London, sealed in a blacked-out compartment, growing increasingly jumpy as we came nearer that city where the wail of sirens and the thud of bombs are as routine every night as supper.

We were running late by now, and consequently couldn't tell exactly how close we were getting to London. The train would stop frequently for several minutes at a time. At these stops we would turn out the light, then pull the blind and look out, trying to see something familiar. George had lived in London for years and he knows the landmarks for miles around.

We could not see anything at all. We. seemed to be out in the country. "We're apparently still a long way off," George said. Then, on the next peek, not two minutes later, he said, "We're here! We're coming into the station!"

We had arrived in the very heart of London before we knew we had even approached the suburbs.

The very first words I heard spoken in London were, "Well, he hasn't come yet, sir, he's more than a bit late tonight."

They were spoken by an aged station porter who opened our compartment door and reached for our bags. The station was lighted so dimly that I could barely see him, but his voice was old — though it had gayness in it too.

What the porter meant was that the Germans had not yet appeared over London this night. They usually arrive as punctually as the hands of a clock. Apparently they take off from fields across the Channel a few minutes before dark and arrive over London a few minutes after dark.

Our porter talked constantly as he carried our bags through the station and to the street. We dogged his heels, for we could barely see and we didn't want to get completely lost in our first few minutes in London.

The porter said, "I had a gentleman a bit ago and he said 'Could I speak with you for a second?' I said 'Yes indeed you may. Time's up.' The gentleman didn't get it at first, and then he thought it was pretty good. You might as well have a bit of a laugh, I guess."

Our station was right in the center of London. It had been hit at least three times, and once a German plane had fallen through the roof. Yet they clean up damage so quickly that we saw no sign of wreckage in the half-light.

In my first night here not a bomb was dropped on London. In fact, not a single German plane appeared over any part of the British Isles that night. Perhaps it was just as well, for if I had arrived in the middle of an inferno of explosion and fire they might have had a berserk American on their hands. Even as it was, those first few minutes in London will be a panorama running before my memory's eye for a lifetime — a panorama more of impressions than of things actually seen.

The night was not entirely black. The moon was up, and you could dimly distinguish shapes if not details. You could see the black outline of a car a few yards away, and buildings stood out against the faint hint of light in the sky.

At the porter's shout a taxi pulled up at the curb and we rumbled off into the darkness. There was very little traffic. Perhaps two cars to a block. Now and then there was a bus. You could see pin points of light moving down the street, but you could get no perspective on them. They were like slowly moving stars in the sky. Then as they came near they would be surrounded by a great black shape, and you could tell it was a bus — but not until you were abreast of it.

As the moon came out fuller it shone on the sides of the buildings and made them appear snow-covered. The city was ghostly silent. Only the low sound of our motor and the small purr of a passing car — that was all. There was no other sound in the streets of London. Yet it wasn't the silence of a graveyard. That wasn't the feeling at all. It was like something mysterious, darkly seen in a dream — shapes here, shadows there, tiny lights swimming toward you, dark bulks moving noiselessly away. And where I had expected to see block after block of vacant spaces and jumbled wreckage, there stood block after block of whole buildings.

I thought to myself: Is this nonsense? Or is London really still here? And I realized there in the dark, with a kind of incredulous excitement, that London was still here, and very much so.

As we drove along in our darkened taxi, Lait pointed things out to me — buildings that we could see only vaguely in the hazy light of the moon. We passed the Houses of Parliament, and saw Big Ben high up there in his tower. But he was not telling the time, either for us or for German fliers; he was all dark. We drove onto Victoria Embankment and along the Thames. We saw Westminster Bridge and a little later Waterloo Bridge. I was astonished to see them still standing. Since then I have found that all the Thames bridges are standing, every one of them open to traffic. We passed the great obelisk called Cleopatra's Needle, which was nicked by bombs from a Zeppelin in the last war but hasn't been touched this time. Then we turned off into a maze of side streets that finally brought us to Fleet Street, the greatest newspaper street in the world. There Lait got out to go to his office, and the cab went on around the corner to my immediate destination.

The driver couldn't locate the number. He yelled at the shadows of some men unloading something from a truck. He yelled at vaguely seen passers-by. Nobody knew where the number was. Finally the driver — and this was the only unpleasant thing I had encountered so far in England — told me to get out and hunt. It seemed that it was not his responsibility to get me there.

I said, "Good Lord, man, I've only been in London ten minutes and I was never here before in my life. How in heaven's name am I going to find anything in this blackout?"

So he groused a little and yelled at some more passers-by and finally did locate the address. I paid him off and carried my bags and sugar sack up to the door. A tiny blue light shone over it. The entire front was packed high with sandbags.

I didn't know whether I dared to enter or not, for fear of letting out light. The tenderfoot treads cautiously in London these nights. He doesn't want to make a fool of himself. But finally I gingerly pulled open the glass door, reached in and touched a heavy curtain, and pulled that aside. There, behind it was a typical office-building lobby, lighted up. I was in the right place.

On an upper floor I found the men of the United Press at work. Their windows were blacked out. Tin hats and gas masks lay thrown on tables. The men were surprised to see a stranger walk in from America unannounced at that time of night.

They gave me suggestions about hotels and made several phone calls for me. All the calls went through immediately, just as though London had never been bombed. And they sent an office boy to dig up another taxi, for not many cabs cruise the streets at night.

We drove a few blocks in the dark and then pulled into what seemed to be an alley. It was as dead and silent and black as a pit.

"I hope I'm not being held up," I thought.

At the end of the alley the taxi made a half turn and stopped. Someone outside opened the door and shone a flashlight on the floor of the taxi. Then I saw that he was a doorman and that we were at the entrance of one of London's finest hotels, the Savoy.

I went through a revolving door, the panes of which were blacked out with cardboard, and stepped into the same luxury and brightness and crowds of people that you can find in any good New York hotel. The reception clerks were all in tuxedos. The bellboys were in gray uniforms. The elevator operators wore wing collars.

I laughed and apologized for my sugar sack, but I needn't have done so. Anything is all right during the "emergency." On my way through the reception room I noticed a man sitting at a table drinking coffee. He was on his way to sleep in the hotel's basement shelter. He was in pajamas and bathrobe.

Imagine sitting in the lobby of the Mayflower in Washington or the Mark Hopkins in San Francisco in pajamas!

Before coming here I knew only one person in this city of eight million. This was Ben Robertson, now London correspondent of PM, the New York newspaper. I hadn't seen him in years, but within forty-five minutes after stepping off the train in London I was shaking hands with Ben Robertson. Talk about being glad to see anybody! It was like striking gold.

I found him in the Savoy dining room eating with two young members of Parliament. One was Dick Law, son of England's famous statesman, Andrew Bonar Law. Dick is financial secretary to the War Office. The other was Jim Thomas, parliamentary secretary to Anthony Eden.

I hadn't eaten a real meal in twenty-four hours. So I ate one now — soup, chicken, mashed potatoes, a green salad, pastry, coffee. You could get practically anything you wanted. The dining room was packed and an orchestra was playing.

Bob Casey of the Chicago Daily News came by, and Larry Rue of the Chicago Tribune. Frank Owen, editor of Lord Beaverbrook's London Standard, came and talked about how things were going for Britain.

My new English friends wanted to know what America thought; and they told queer bomb stories by the dozen. "You're a welcome sight," they said. "We've all told our bomb stories to each other so many times that nobody listens any more. Now we've got a new audience."

What an introduction to London! I not only felt vastly relieved to be among friends, but also as snug as a bug and as big as a barrage balloon. To say nothing of feeling extremely brave, since there were no planes over England that night.

It was midnight when I got to bed. It was the first bed I had lain in for forty hours.

Everything was wonderful. "This can't last," I said to myself. "This isn't the way the people live." But it's mighty good for your soul on your first night in London.

My first two days were consumed in getting signed up and identified. Now I have so many papers that I've had to buy an extra wallet, a leather case so big I have to carry it in a side pocket, and it is already stuffed full.

First you register with the police and get a booklet with your picture in it. You have to give them your whole life history. If you move, they must be notified.

Then there is the national registration. Here you get another booklet — and don't you lose it! Then you get your food-ration book. Then you report to the Ministry of Information and get a pass with your picture on it. Then the ministry gives additional cards permitting you to stay out after midnight and enter prohibited areas, such as zones of military action.

3. FIRST IMPRESSIONS

London,
December, 1940.

Everywhere you go people are nice to you. At the police station it took half an hour to get my business done because a policeman had to tell me about the bombs in his neighborhood. I have never seen policemen at home so friendly and helpful. And it wasn't just because I was an American. For I watched them at other desks, where other foreigners were registering, and these got the same courteous treatment.

My particular policeman lives in a quiet suburb on a rise of ground, with a good view. And he said that the night before I arrived London was a sight to see, with searchlights and noise and fires all over town. He said a bomb hit his block not long ago and wiped out thirteen houses. But only five people were hurt and nobody was killed.

"Imagine bombing a quiet, homey suburb like ours!" he said. "What military advantage could that possibly have?"

"Well," I said, "I suppose the point is to try to break the spirit of the people."

And he said, not boastfully but in an ordinary tone, "I guess so; but actually it's having just the opposite effect."

I asked him if he had a backyard shelter. He said he did, but never went into it. He preferred to sleep in his own bed, get a good rest and take his chances.

On my second afternoon here I got a haircut. The barber talked all the time, and for once I enjoyed it. He knew instantly that I was an American. We don't look very different to me, but these Londoners can tell an American a mile off. It didn't take the barber long to find out that I had just arrived and that my first two nights in London had passed without a single bomb being dropped. He said we'd have some before many nights.

"And I'll tell you " he said, "if you don't get a little windy your first night, then you're not much of a man. A fellow who doesn't get his wind up at the first experience isn't a man at all. He's just an animal with no nerves in his body."

I told the barber I was all prepared to be London's biggest coward. He said not to be ashamed if I was scared and did something silly. He was an air-raid warden at night in his home suburb, he said, and what did I suppose he did in their very first raid? He dived for the nearest underground shelter. When he got down there, he said, he realized that was no place for a warden to be, and he was so ashamed he took off his badge so people wouldn't know he was a warden.

But that was soon changed. Now his whole district is organized. They know exactly what to expect and what to do, and they go about it like a business. He goes to his post every night after supper. Every third night he is on duty all night, regardless of whether anything happens. On other nights he stays on if things are happening. He's not afraid any more at all.

I'm mighty glad I got a haircut. The barber was a great solace. Before that talk I had been afraid of bombs, and also afraid to have anyone know I was afraid. Now I'm only afraid of bombs.

I had heard stories of new arrivals over here sleeping right through their first air-raid warning, but I never thought anything so drab would happen to me. It did.

This morning at nine-thirty a friend came to my room. "Did you hear the warning?" he asked. "Don't make fun of me," I said. "There wasn't any warning." But he was right. The sirens went off at 6 a.m. There was just one plane over town, and it didn't drop anything. The all clear sounded at 6:30, and I slept through that too.

I think the English bed manufacturers should have me write a testimonial.

In my first few days here I have met an enormous number of people. The first thing everyone says — and I'll bet I've heard it two hundred times — is this:

"Is it better or worse than you thought it would be?"

Then I have to explain to them that in the United States we had felt that perhaps, because of the censorship, we might not be getting a complete picture of the devastation. We had been afraid that London was more grievously wounded than we were being allowed to know. And now, having been prepared for any shock and having looked at London, I can truthfully answer that it is better off than I had expected.

I think the newspapers have given a proper estimate of the damage. True, the destruction has been immense. But these ghastly blows actually have hurt London less than it is possible to imagine or believe without seeing for yourself.

London as a living, enduring institution is not gravely injured. Not in its architecture, or in its mode of existence, or its utilities, or its transportation, or its health. And above all, not in its spirit. So far, the blitz on London is a failure. London is no more knocked out than the man who smashes a finger is dead. Daytime life in London today comes very close to being normal.

My reply of "better" seemed to please the questioners, with one exception. A girl said, "Oh, I'm sorry to hear you say that." I think she probably felt that I didn't appreciate what they had been through. Also, she may have thought that if I wrote such stuff back to the States it might lead people to believe that Britain didn't need help as badly as she really does.

There are no restrictions on newspapermen here. They can travel wherever they like.

The two sections of London hardest hit are the poor East End and the rich West End. The latter would correspond to the Times Square and Fifth Avenue districts in New York; or to all of downtown Washington between the Capitol and the "Million Dollar" Bridge; or to San Francisco from Market Street to Russian Hill.

I haven't been to the East End yet, but I have walked at least ten miles through the West End. I covered and re-covered the Parliament Buildings, Regent and Oxford Streets (the great shopping centers). Pall Mall and Piccadilly, Park Lane and Leicester Square, the Strand and Holborn Circus. And the best way I can describe it is to say this:

You may walk a block or two without seeing a single wrecked building. Then occasionally you will see a block that is half wiped out. But the typical block in the West End would have perhaps two buildings completely wrecked by bomb or fire, and half a dozen damaged but not destroyed. That still leaves a lot of whole, sound buildings.

There is in the West End no single great sweep of destruction, with everything flat — just a building damaged here and another there.

You are impressed when you see how little effect a bomb has on a building unless it is a bomb of the very heaviest type. A big modern building next door to us took a heavy bomb right on top, yet it stands there today whole and beautiful, only slightly damaged. Steel and concrete and stone usually stand up. It is the age-weary buildings of brick and dry mortar that have gone down in heart-sickening heaps.

Much of the damage is not visible to a person walking on the street. I was in a plant, the rear part of which had been blown to the ground, yet from the front it looked untouched. A house next door to doom may get nothing more than broken windows. The Savoy Hotel stands up as big as life, but it has been hit more than once. The famous Savoy Grill is closed while bomb damage is repaired. And when I was taking a gander out my window I discovered that the room next to mine was unoccupied — because a bomb had blown off a corner of it.

Yet the service — food, light, drink, attention — goes on as usual, even to the floor porter complaining that I hadn't put my shoes out for him to shine. The British won't let anything interfere with their being British.

The damage is terrific, but what impresses me most about it — and the point I want to get over — is this: it doesn't make any difference!

That sounds heartless. But honestly, it's the way the British look at it. They don't feel that they have been hurt at all.

An American who has been here through it all says the most impressive thing to him is the way people who have been secure have abandoned their property sense. They can see their buildings go up in smoke, their savings blasted to bits, and apparently they don't care — so long as "we get that guy in the end."

PART III: MOST HATEFUL, MOST BEAUTIFUL

1. RINGED AND STABBED WITH FIRE

London,
December, 1940.

Some day when peace has returned to this odd world I want to come to London again and stand on a certain balcony on a moonlit night and look down upon the peaceful silver curve of the Thames with its dark bridges. And standing there, I want to tell somebody who has never seen it how London looked on a certain night in the holiday season of the year 1940.

For on that night this old, old city was — even though I must bite my tongue in shame for saying it — the most beautiful sight I have ever seen.

It was a night when London was ringed and stabbed with fire.

They came just after dark, and somehow you could sense from the quick, bitter firing of the guns that there was to be no monkey business this night.

Shortly after the sirens wailed you could hear the Germans grinding overhead. In my room, with its black curtains drawn across the windows, you could feel the shake from the guns. You could hear the boom, crump, crump, crump, of heavy bombs at their work of tearing buildings apart. They were not too far away.

Half an hour after the firing started I gathered a couple of friends and went to a high, darkened balcony that gave us a view of a third of the entire circle of London. As we stepped out onto the balcony a vast inner excitement came over all of us — an excitement that had neither fear nor horror in it, because it was too full of awe.

You have all seen big fires, but I doubt if you have ever seen the whole horizon of a city lined with great fires — scores of them, perhaps hundreds.

There was something inspiring just in the awful savagery of it.

The closest fires were near enough for us to hear the crackling flames and the yells of firemen. Little fires grew into big ones even as we watched. Big ones died down under the firemen's valor, only to break out again later.

About every two minutes a new wave of planes would be over. The motors seemed to grind rather than roar, and to have an angry pulsation, like a bee buzzing in blind fury.

The guns did not make a constant overwhelming din as in those terrible days of September. They were intermittent — sometimes a few seconds apart, sometimes a minute or more. Their sound was sharp, near by; and soft and muffled, far away. They were everywhere over London.

Into the dark shadowed spaces below us, while we watched, whole batches of incendiary bombs fell. We saw two dozen go off in two seconds. They flashed terrifically, then quickly simmered down to pin points of dazzling white, burning ferociously. These white pin points would go out one by one, as the unseen heroes of the moment smothered them with sand. But also, while we watched, other pin points would burn on, and soon a yellow flame would leap up from the white center. They had done their work — another building was on fire.

The greatest of all the fires was directly in front of us. Flames seemed to whip hundreds of feet into the air. Pinkish-white smoke ballooned upward in a great cloud, and out of this cloud there gradually took shape — so faintly at first that we weren't sure we saw correctly — the gigantic dome of St. Paul's Cathedral.

St. Paul's was surrounded by fire, but it came through. It stood there in its enormous proportions — growing slowly clearer and clearer, the way objects take shape at dawn. It was like a picture of some miraculous figure that appears before peace-hungry soldiers on a battlefield.

The streets below us were semi-illuminated from the glow. Immediately above the fires the sky was red and angry, and overhead, making a ceiling in the vast heavens, there was a cloud of smoke all in pink. Up in that pink shrouding there were tiny, brilliant specks of flashing light — antiaircraft shells bursting. After the flash you could hear the sound.

Up there, too, the barrage balloons were standing out as clearly as if it were daytime, but now they were pink instead of silver. And now and then through a hole in that pink shroud there twinkled incongruously a permanent, genuine star — the old-fashioned kind that has always been there.

Below us the Thames grew lighter, and all around below were the shadows — the dark shadows of buildings and bridges that formed the base of this dreadful masterpiece.

Later on I borrowed a tin hat and went out among the fires. That was exciting too; but the thing I shall always remember above all the other things in my life is the monstrous loveliness of that one single view of London on a holiday night — London stabbed with great fires, shaken by explosions, its dark regions along the Thames sparkling with the pin points of white-hot bombs, all of it roofed over with a ceiling of pink that held bursting shells, balloons, flares and the grind of vicious engines. And in yourself the excitement and anticipation and wonder in your soul that this could be happening at all.

These things all went together to make the most hateful, most beautiful single scene I have ever known.

2. NIGHT STROLL, ILLUMINATED

London,
December, 1940.

London learns a lesson from each new horror that the Germans bring over.

Through the school of experience it is gradually acquiring a superb efficiency at its new career of bomb-receiving. It learned a keen lesson from that Sunday night fire-bombing which was my own introduction to modern war. That lesson was that the rooftops of London must be manned through every hour of darkness.

They say there are a million buildings in London. Of course there is not a watcher on every single little roof; but hereafter whenever Hitler sends his fire-sprayers there will be at least a quarter of a million pairs of hands and eyes waiting on the darkened rooftops to smother his fire bombs or direct the firemen to them.

Let me tell you how an incendiary bomb works.

A fire bomb is about a foot long, and shaped like a miniature torpedo. On the upper end are three metal fins circled by a strip of metal on top. The bomb is made of a magnesium alloy, with a thermite core. Each one weighs a little better than two pounds. One plane can scatter a thousand of them. Ten planes could easily start 750 fires at once, over a large area.

Of course you don't see the bombs falling. They go off when they strike. If they hit the street they bounce crazily like a football, sputter violently for the first minute, throwing white fire about thirty feet, and then simmer down in an intense molten mass and burn about ten minutes more. It is said they burn at a temperature of 2000 degrees. If one is left on a floor it will burn a hole and drop through. When they land in the open they are easily smothered with sand. Common ordinary citizens have smothered thousands of them.

Sunday night I saw one that fell within two feet of an emergency sandbox in the street. That was an easy one. But few of them land so conveniently.

That night I went to an office building which I visit frequently, and there two fire bombs had plunged through the roof and on down through three floors. One of them had gone through a heavy sheet of steel laid over an airshaft. It left an opening in that steel plate exactly the shape of the bomb, and as neat as though it had been cut in cardboard with a knife.

Now there was a lesson about placing roof spotters. The men on the roof of that building knew that those bombs had gone through, and they were quickly smothered. But there were hundreds of unwatched buildings in London that night into which fire bombs plunged unnoticed, and ten minutes later the buildings were aflame.

That night as I wandered along Fleet Street I saw a five-story building suddenly leap into great flames. The firemen hadn't even known there was a fire in it.

At home, when a big fire starts, the police rope off the whole section, but it wasn't so in London Sunday night. What few pedestrians there were could go anywhere they liked, and they didn't have to feel their way that night, for there was no darkness.

Probably foolishly, I walked down a street that was afire on both sides, past walls that would soon be ready to fall. Hundreds of small motor pumps, carried in two-wheeled trailers behind cars, stood in the streets. The engines made such a whir you couldn't have heard a plane overhead. Firemen by the hundreds were working calmly, shouting orders to each other, smoking cigarettes, and paying no attention to pedestrians.

I walked ten blocks. Every step had to be picked carefully amid an intertwined mass of fire hose.

Somehow I didn't have a feeling that this was war. I just felt as if I were seeing a terrific number of big "natural" fires. Even when I came upon two buildings that had been blown to dust by heavy bombs less than an hour before, there was still a feeling that it was all perfectly "natural."

Although bombs are liable to fall anywhere, it happened that none came within six blocks of where we stood watching the early part of the fantastic show Sunday night. There were fires all around us, but we seemed to be on an island of immunity.

When we started out among the fires, the friends with whom I had been watching took another route and I did my fire-wandering alone. Oddly enough, I was never afraid. As I remember it, my only concern was lest I get in the firemen's way.

When I returned to our oasis shortly before midnight, just as I stepped in the door the "raiders passed" signal sounded. Up in my room I discovered that my feet were soaked and my coat drenched with spray from leaky hoses.

When I turned out the light and pulled the blackout curtains from across the windows the room was bright from the glare of the fires, and it was hard to get to sleep. But I did sleep. And when I awakened, about six o'clock in the morning, the great light in the sky was gone. London again was almost as dark as it has been every night for a year and a half. So well do the firemen of London do their work.

The coming of daylight is always a blessing. Things have a way of looking overly grotesque at night. Today I can go out onto our balcony, where we stood watching London burn, and London will look just as it did the afternoon before the raiders came. True, property was destroyed — much property, valuable both materially and sentimentally. And lives were lost. But London is big, and its lives are many. You feel a little abashed to realize the next morning that London is still here. The skyline looks just the same. The streets are jammed with human beings.

Life is going on — where last night you felt that this must be the end of everything.

3. THE LANDMARKS

London,
January, 1941.

Let us go for a walk on the tourist beat — or what was the tourist beat in the days when tourists could come to London.

We see that Westminster Abbey has been hit. Its beautiful windows have been knocked out. But ninety-eight per cent of the building is still there, and it is still open to visitors. Today I stood over the small new block of concrete in the floor that covers Mr. Chamberlain's grave, the Abbey's latest.

It is darkish in the Abbey now, for most of the windows are boarded up.

Parliament? Yes, these buildings have been hit. But again it is a case of a smashed finger, not a fatal injury. The entrance to the House of Commons is gone; there is some damage to the interior; and the same bomb damaged the rear end of Richard the Lionhearted's bronze horse and bent Richard's upheld sword, but he still rides on.

This one amuses me: Before the war started, the great tower above the House of Lords was shrouded by a maze of steel scaffolding, in connection with a wide plan for remodeling and repair. So what did they do? They went right ahead repairing.

And Big Ben? Well, he's still striking the hours. He hasn't been touched, despite half a dozen German claims that he has been knocked down.

Bombs have fallen around Trafalgar Square, yet Nelson still stands atop his great monument, and the immortal British lions, all four of them, still crouch at the base of the statue, untouched.

The statues of Lincoln and Washington have not been hit. You can still get roast beef at Simpson's (and you still tip the chef sixpence when he wheels it to your table and cuts off a slice). If you had a favorite pub, ten to one it is still serving ale.

With two exceptions, all the well-known hotels are still operating, and are full. The exceptions are the Carlton and another that I can't name. The Carlton was burned, but they say it is going to be repaired and reopened.

The big hotels have music and dancing as usual. The lounges are utterly packed at teatime with tea and coffee drinkers. The only difference from peacetime is that you can't see your hand in front of you when you walk out the front door at night.

St. Paul's Cathedral has been hit in the rear but the damage is not nearly as bad as I had heard. The cathedral as a whole is still there, and it is open. The damaged wing is shut off by a gate, on which a sign says, not "No Admittance," but "Out of Bounds."

The people of London are both philosophical and proud about St. Paul's. They go to look at it without sadness, and they say, "We would rather have it that way in a free London than have it whole like Notre Dame in an imprisoned Paris."

The Tower of London has been hit, and a bomb struck near the Bank of England. But both places still stand. The Natural History Museum has been bombed, and what many people consider a wonderful joke was a direct hit on the million-year-old skeleton of a brontosaurus.

Londoners pray daily that a German bomb will do something about the Albert Memorial in Kensington Gardens. If you have ever seen it, you know why. As the British say, they could bear its removal with equanimity. But the contrary Germans have only taken a few little chips out of it.

Madame Tussaud's Waxworks is open again, after being temporarily closed by a bombing next door. There are bomb craters in all the familiar parks. The American Express office in Haymarket has not been touched, although buildings have been wrecked near by.

Some months ago Vincent Sheean had a piece in the Redbook magazine describing the chaotic wreckage in the West End. I remember specifically his picture of how Oxford Street was blocked off and deserted and ankle-deep in broken glass and rubble. Friends of mine were along when Sheean did his reporting for that piece, and they say he gave a true picture. But he would be surprised to see Oxford Street now.

It is as wide open as ever, jammed with buses and packed with pedestrians. In fact, it looks about like F Street in Washington the week before Christmas. Nearly all the stores are open. True, I could count on my hands the stores left with their original windows. But losing windows doesn't cause a building to fall down. Business goes on as usual.

Selfridge's famous department store is standing, and is open. The great Lewis store burned to the ground, as you may have seen in the newsreels — they say this was London's second biggest fire — but Lewis' rented all the ground-floor shops in the next block and is open again. Incidentally, Lewis' gave London an awful shock the day after the fire, for they carried ads in the papers saying they knew their customers would be pleased to learn that a duplicate set of their books had been removed to the country beforehand, and consequently they had a complete record of the bills owed them.

All in all, it seems to me that London's tourist beat has escaped remarkably well.

Just the same, a few minutes' walk will show you that this is a city at war.

Every block is dotted with shelter signs. The official ones are black metal plates clamped to lamp posts, like street signs. They have a big white letter "S," and underneath in small letters the word "Shelter" and a white arrow pointing to the building in front of which the sign is affixed. Each sign has a little V-shaped roof over it to keep the dim night-light from shining upward.

Every block has a dozen signs of white paper, pasted on building walls, saying "Shelter Here During Business Hours" or "Shelter for Fifty Persons after 5 p.m." A shelter is anything that protects you. It may be an underground restaurant, a store basement, a bank vault.

I know buildings in London that go six stories underground. When the banshee wails in London's West End you wouldn't have to run fifty yards in any direction to find a shelter.

Other signs, in yellow and black, say "To the Trenches." They point the way to shelters dug underneath small downtown parks such as Leicester Square. Every park and open space in London's West End has a newly built catacomb underneath.

Then there are surface shelters. You see these everywhere. They are simply long, windowless, flat-topped sheds, about 8 feet high and 10 feet wide, stretching for a block or more. They are built of a light-tan brick and are divided into sections, each of which will hold about fifty persons. Some of them are built right down the middle of wide streets. Others are on sidewalks, up against the buildings, leaving only a couple of feet of sidewalk room.

There are also signs with arrows pointing to first-aid posts and fire substations.

All over London, in little parks and areaways and alleys there are tanks of water for fire-fighting. Barrels and buckets of sand, for throwing on incendiary bombs, small pumps and auxiliary fire apparatus are scattered everywhere. Even in the halls of my hotel.

A colossal amount of construction and repair work is going on all over London. Thirty-five thousand men are engaged in cleaning up the rubble of bombed buildings. Other scores of thousands work on the streets and under them on the maze of utility pipes and wires. Thousands more dig, build and hammer day and night, including Sundays, making more deep shelters, bricking up window openings, throwing up auxiliary walls.

Many a building has a brick wall standing in the middle of the sidewalk about three feet in front of its entrance, with a door in the middle. A few have built brick walls that entirely blanket their store fronts. And in some of London's most important buildings workmen today are bricking up every window opening, leaving only one little gunhole in the center. This is for the invasion, if it ever comes and if it gets this far. Of course nobody believes that it will get this far, but they are taking no chances. They are making ready to fight in every street, behind every wall, out of every window, if it must come to that.

Around some Government buildings there are nasty-looking mazes of barbed wire. Some of the public statues are completely buried under mounds of sandbags, but most of them aren't.

Piles of sandbags buttress the foundations of thousands of stores. Many of these sandbag piles look ragged and ratty now, for the bags have sprung leaks from long exposure to the weather, and sand trickles out of them. Many of them, for that matter, have been stabbed by fire fighters getting sand to put out incendiary bombs.

Army cars run about the streets. Huge, streamlined buses, camouflaged with a dull brown paint, come to town with soldiers on leave. You could hardly count the pedestrians in one block who are in uniform. At the cheaper restaurants the checkroom has more rifles than umbrellas.

Occasionally in some open space you see a flat sheet of brass-colored metal on top of a waist-high post. It looks something like a sun dial. This is a gas detector. If gas ever comes, this metal will change color.

Great parks are all dug up with trenches and mounds of dirt to keep enemy planes from landing. St. James's Park has its honorable bomb craters, and its below-ground shelters, and even its barbed wire. Occasionally you see a big gun on a rooftop.

All this panorama is in addition to the wreckage you see on every side.

Yes, London is a martial city. You can hardly conceive of Denver or Indianapolis looking like it. And yet people are so accustomed to it now that they seem hardly to notice anything different from normal. Nobody, unless he is brand-new here, stops to look at bomb damage. Londoners seem barely aware of the barbed wire, the dugouts, the shelter signs. And I found that I, too, after a few days, could walk block after block without particularly noticing any of these things.

It is a new type of life; and that life has now become, through months of living with it, the normal life.

4. ROUGHING IT

London,
January, 1941.

Some very wrong things were told me in America about the way I would have to live in London.

I was told that even in the best hotels you could get hot water only one day a week; that you couldn't get laundry done, so you would have to throw away your soiled shirts and buy new ones; that you couldn't buy any new ones; that there would be no decent hotel rooms; that you could get only one egg a week, and no tea; that food was so scarce it would be wise to bring concentrated food tablets and beef bouillon cubes.

Well, you ought to see where I'm staying. My room is the last word in good taste. It is completely modern and comfortable. There are deep chairs, and a bed that is a dream. I have two telephones, and a waiter, maid and valet who come when I ring. My bathroom is as big as an ordinary room, and the water is scalding hot twenty-four hours a day. Above all, the radiator gives off real heat. I'm as warm as I would be at home.

On my first morning here I asked if it would be possible to get an egg for breakfast. I not only got an egg — they brought me two eggs, ham, toast, jam and coffee, and they've been bringing the same thing every morning. Honestly, I feel ashamed to eat it. Of course only a tiny portion of London's population is living like this. My circumstances do not give anything like a true picture of how England is living today. But my life now is at least a true picture of how it is possible to live in London if you pay the price. And the price I pay the hotel is $6 a day, which includes breakfast.

All this makes it hard to realize a war is actually going on. But then, there are things around the hotel that remind you.

Over the big windows of my room, looking out onto the Strand, hang thick, heavily padded curtains. On the street side these are black; on the room side, brown satin. Instead of being an unsightly makeshift, they are beautiful. Hanging on them is a card warning me not to open the curtains during the blackout under any circumstances. I was so apprehensive about doing something I shouldn't that I slept all that first night without opening a window. I slept soundly, too, but naturally I was groggy in the morning. So I asked a clerk what to do about ventilation at night. He said, "Why, as soon as you turn out the lights, go and open the curtains and the window too. It's all right just so you don't show a, light during the night."

So you see I'm slow to catch on, but I'd rather be slow than dead.

The hotel's big dining room has been moved to a lower floor, the better to keep away from the bombs. Here the waiters are all in formal clothes, an orchestra plays, and bellboys hurry about calling people to the telephone. You'd hardly know there was a war except that half the hats in the checkroom are tin hats, half the diners are in uniform, and hanging from the great center chandelier is an old-fashioned kerosene lantern, just in case.

On each table stands a handsomely printed card which says: "This room is provided with special protection from blast and splinters. The inner wall is 14 inches thick. The outer wall, five feet distant, is nine inches thick. The brick joints in each wall are strengthened with steel mesh, and the two walls support each other by 16 connecting steel rods. There are nine floors, of steel construction, above this room. The air-raid shelter is immediately below."

But about those other warnings I had before leaving America. I have sent out my laundry and my coat to be cleaned, and they will be back tomorrow. They'd be back this evening if I wanted to pay extra.

As for shirts, I could buy any number of them, and heavy underwear, socks, suits, coats and everything else any human being could think of to wrap around his body or hang upon it. In fact, the store windows are so entrancing that I'm buying sweaters and coats and things I don't need at all, just because they are so good-looking.

And about the concentrated food pills. Well, I haven't wanted anything to eat yet that I couldn't get, except enough sugar.

I have heard that paper is running short, but yesterday I bought 500 sheets of the same kind of writing paper I use at home, and at two-thirds the usual price.

Lastly, about those beef cubes I should have brought. Apparently the national drink in England is a beef extract called Bovril, which is advertised everywhere, like Coca Cola at home. Yesterday I went into a snack bar for some lunch. I asked the waitress just what this Bovril stuff was, and in a cockney accent that would lay you in the aisle she said:

"Why sir, it's beef juice and it's wonderful for you on cold days like this. It's expensive, but it's body-buildin', sir, it's very body-buildin'."

So I had a cup. It cost five cents, and you just ought to see my body being built.

5. WHOOO-ISSSHHH!

London,
January, 1941.

Although I've had my big night of fire and plenty of bombs too, I have not yet achieved any intimate acquaintance with a bomb. And I'm quite willing to have the introduction filed under "things pending."

I've heard plenty of bombs explode at a distance, and I've even felt the building I was in shake, but I have yet to go through that horrible experience of hearing a bomb whistling right down toward me. Just the same, I've had this weak old heart stopped once. It didn't happen on our big night of fires. It happened before that.

During your first few days in London you are all at sea. You are tense and jumpy and expectant, waiting and wondering how you will feel when you get your first bad scare. Well, one night I was awakened by the guns about 2 A.M. They kept firing off and on for about an hour, and then stopped.

London was black and silent. There was no sound of any kind anywhere. I just lay in the bed staring at nothing.

And then there was a small, muffled thud in the distance. I ducked under the covers and waited for an explosion. But it never came.

Just that single ghostly "whooo-isshhh" and thud in the darkness, and then hours of silence. It took me a good while to get to sleep again.

The next morning I described it to a friend and asked what on earth it was, or whether I was just hearing things. And he said, "Why, no; that was a piece of falling shrapnel."

I suppose there isn't an American newspaperman in London who lived through the terrifying raids of August and September, 1940, who has not been under the bed at least twice when the bombs were whistling and dropping all around.

Everyone I have talked to, without exception, says it's not so bad if you're with somebody, but you have an absolute horror of being alone. Also, believe it or not, there is a general horror of being caught in the toilet or in the bathtub.

I was alone in my room the first night I actually heard German planes overhead. I was sitting at a desk writing when I heard the great drone of the motors. For several seconds it didn't sink into my consciousness that they were not peaceful motors such as I might hear over Washington or Los Angeles, but were German motors over London. And then, I remember, I was furious because not a single antiaircraft gun was firing.

"Good Lord!" I thought. "They're right over the hotel. I can hear them even with the windows shut. Why don't those guys with the guns do something?"

A minute or so later the guns did start.

The planes were probably a great deal higher than I thought. But I could still almost swear they were no more than three or four thousand feet up. If they dropped any bombs, though, none of them fell near us.

The sound of the motors faded out, but intermittent firing went on for an hour. Then once again I heard planes overhead.

I couldn't keep my mind on my writing. I sat on the edge of the chair, ready to jump down behind the bed if I heard a bomb whistling. But the funniest thing, when I look back on it, is to remember going around the room straightening up everything. I remember laying out on the desk coins and cigarettes and matches and my door key and knife, all in a meticulous row. I had just bought ten packs of cigarettes, and I stacked these neatly. All the letters on the desk I arranged in regimented stacks. I put a flashlight and a jar of Vick's salve in a perfect line with the letters and cigarettes.

At the time I didn't even know I was doing it. It was just a nervous outlet of some kind. When I finally went to bed I suddenly realized what I'd been doing, and laughed at myself.

This hotel has one of the finest basement shelters in London, but none of the American newspapermen who stop at the hotel ever sleeps in the shelter. I haven't slept there yet either. In fact, I find lots of Londoners who prefer to stay in their own beds.

The other day we went out to look at some new bomb damage a couple of miles away. The destruction was ghastly. As we stood and looked, one newspaper veteran of the Battle of Britain said:

"You see, you never know where it's going to hit, and neither does the guy six miles up there in the dark who lets it loose. Just think, if he pressed the trigger at the particular time that would get you, what would be the use of hiding? The chances of any certain bomb having your number on it are very slim, but if it has, running and ducking won't help."

As another newspaperman said, "Your best protection is the law of averages."

6. SOUNDS AND SIGHTS

London,
January, 1941.

Before leaving the United States I told friends that one of the things I wanted to do over here was to try to describe what the air-raid sirens sound like.

Well, I will try to do it. They don't sound quite like a fire-engine siren, although they're on the same principle. The tone has more of the old-fashioned automobile Klaxon in it, except that at the same time, instead of being harsh or squawky, it has an almost musical quality.

The siren sounds one minute for an alert, two minutes for the all clear. On an alert, the sound goes from a low to a high pitch, up and down every few seconds. The result is, if you aren't close to it, it sounds much like a train whistling for a crossing — except that it just keeps on whistling for one crossing after another.

The sirens are scattered all over London. They are roughly fifteen blocks apart. An alert usually starts in the south part of London, you can hear the sirens to the south of you, then all around you, and then beyond to the north. It is like a series of great sound waves washing over the city. These waves overlap; and the time from the moment you hear the first one until the last one within range of your ears is silent may not be more than four minutes.

If you're indoors, the sirens do not seem loud. In fact, during my first few days here I didn't hear them half the time. But when your ear gets attuned to them, you know it the second they start. My hotel isn't close enough to any sirens for them to be annoying, however, or to wake me up if I'm asleep.

I had wondered whether the sirens kept going throughout a raid. They don't. They sound the warning and then are silent until the all clear — and the silent interval may be anywhere from ten minutes to all night. The all clear is announced by the same sirens, but instead of going up and down they go steadily for two minutes in the same tone.

To me, the sirens do not sound fiendish, or even weird. I think they're sort of pretty.

The other night when the all clear sounded I lay on the bed listening. You could hear half a dozen sirens going at once, on exactly the same pitch. The combined whirring of these great horns out there in the still darkness gave off a sort of musical pulsation. In fact, it sounded exactly like the lonely singing of telephone wires on a bitter cold night in the prairies of the Middle West.

Now, what do the guns sound like?

Well, they sound like thunder in a violent electrical storm. When they are very close they sound as though lightning were striking within a quarter of a mile. They shake the floor and rattle the windows. Then as other guns start up, farther and farther away across the city, they sound like thunder traveling away from you.

In reading about the terrific noise of the sirens and guns in the great raids of September, 1940, I often wondered just how close you would be to the nearest anti-aircraft gun. Well, they are all around you. The farthest one might be only a mile from you.

People living in the neighborhood of one of these guns come to have a possessive feeling about it. They call it "my gun," and tell stories about it to their friends. And they get quite annoyed if it's moved away.

In these last few weeks London has, with some outstanding exceptions, been fairly quiet, while the Germans have been giving one-night blitzes to other English cities. But a great many of the raiders pass right over London, terrifically high, on their way north.

Our sirens sound a warning, apparently when the Germans cross the coastline, usually about six o'clock in the evening. Then about fifteen minutes later, our guns start up. They shoot sporadically for an hour or so, and then all is quiet. Sometimes the all clear is sounded at this point, but more often not. For usually there is shooting again around 11 p.m. and 2 a.m., and the all clear ordinarily sounds about three o'clock.

The guns naturally waken you and keep you awake. But more often than not I am sound asleep when the all clear tells besieged London that it can relax once more.

You've read about the barrage balloons over London. Their purpose, as you know, is to keep German fliers high, from fear of running into them.

At night they are floated into the sky at the end of thin steel cables. The balloons are silver-colored and shaped like very fat sausages; and they have pudgy stabilizing fins at one end that make them look like Walt Disney elephants with sour but coy faces.

I had supposed that these balloon cables made a great wall around London, with the balloons themselves forming the top of this wall. But that isn't the way at all. Instead of making a border they run up all over London, like candles on an eighty-year-old's birthday cake.

When the weather is clear you can look up and see a couple of dozen of them from any spot. They are floating at various altitudes, seemingly about half a mile apart, and not in line. They're just scattered up there, and they look more like a ceiling than a wall.

As proof of how little the average person looks toward the sky, I have thought to look at the balloons only two or three times since coming here, and friends of mine say they haven't noticed them for weeks.

Suppose, I asked, a German plane should run into a balloon cable and cut it in two. Englishmen can't do the old Hindu rope trick; so consequently all those miles of free cable up in the sky would have to come down. What happens then?

Well, it comes down all right, and plenty happens. The cable folds and wraps itself around buildings all over its particular section of town. This doesn't happen often, but when it does I would just as soon be elsewhere.

On New Year's Day I took a long walk through Hyde Park and Kensington Gardens. Believe it or not, there amid the trenches and the bomb craters and in the raw, cold weather was a whole garden of red and yellow roses in bloom.

A single bombing is referred to in London, with traditional British reserve, as an "incident." If you ask a bobby where that big one went off last night he is apt to say, "Two blocks ahead, a block to the left, turn right, and you will be at the scene of the incident."

When you get there, the "incident" will likely turn out to be half a block merely blown all to hell.

The other day we saw a fire engine dashing madly down the street. There had been no alert, and no enemy planes were over the city. The engine was simply going to an ordinary old-fashioned fire. It seemed absolutely incongruous. We had forgotten that fires had been starting without bombs for centuries, and that fire engines had been running to them in peacetime for generations.

Antiaircraft guns, they tell me, can propel a shell upward for better than four miles. The shells are set to explode at a given altitude; or rather, a given number of seconds after leaving the gun. When they explode they make a great flash, and fragments are thrown over a radius of several hundred yards. Thus they don't have to get a direct hit on a plane, which would be more accidental than anything else. If they just get somewhere near him the explosion will sure make him jump.

But what goes up must come down. The falling pieces of these exploded shells are shrapnel. And if you get hit by a small piece of steel that has fallen four miles you are going to get hurt. Hence the tin hat or steel helmet.

Every man in uniform carries a steel helmet and a gas mask on a strap over his shoulder. Even when on leave, men in the services are obliged to carry them constantly. The rule is so strict that if a soldier gets hit by shrapnel when not wearing his tin hat, then the injury is considered a self-inflicted wound and he is disciplined accordingly.

But the people of London themselves have relaxed. Today on the streets you don't see one civilian in five hundred carrying either a tin hat or a gas mask. In fact, real steel helmets are all gone. It is impossible to buy one. But the stores are selling helmets made of a heavy black fiber composition. They say these work just about as well as the tin ones. I bought one the other day for three dollars, and within four hours I had forgotten it and left it somewhere. So now I either have to shell out another three bucks, or run the chance of going around covered with self-inflicted wounds. I can't decide what to do.

7. BLINDFOLDED IN SAHARA

London,
January, 1941.

Now the days are getting longer, and the people of London count the few precious minutes of added daylight each day as though they were pearls.

For truly the blackout is a heavy and insidious thing. It gradually gets on your nerves until you feel as if you must throw it aside and let the light out into the night. Modern man is not attuned to natural darkness.

Every day the papers publish the exact minute for blacking out. When I first came to London the nights were at their very longest. The blackout went on as early as 5:19 p.m. and didn't end until 8:35 in the morning. That's more than fifteen hours of blackness.

It is a finable offense to show a light from a window during the blackout. You don't even dare to light a cigarette in the street.

One morning a friend of mine, who is stopping in the same hotel, opened his curtains at 8:25. His watch was fast and he didn't know it. In just one minute a plane spotter on a near-by roof had sent a man to knock on his door and suggest that he be more careful in the future.

Every afternoon about four a maid comes to my room and asks if she may "black out now." But we have made an arrangement for me to take advantage of the outdoor light as long as possible, and then close the curtains myself about five o'clock.

Some friends of mine live m an apartment. Just before I came here London had a hot and heavy night, with incendiary and high-explosive bombs falling over the entire city. Apparently my friends were showing a little light, for a warden came and warned them. And not a minute after he had left, two or three bombs dropped within a block or so.

The warden came back and said: "Now you see? The Germans saw your light. That's why we're getting these bombs here now."

Of course he really didn't think that, but it made a good joke. The best "joke," however, was that when the warden continued his rounds he discovered that those two bombs he was talking about had blown his own house to smithereens.

A few nights ago a warden knocked on my door and said a plane spotter across the street had seen a light in my window. The warden inspected the curtains and said they were perfectly all right. But about two hours later he was back, saying the spotter still reported a light from my window.

We finally figured out that a desk light on my writing table was shining up toward the top of the curtains, and that a little light was seeping through. So I moved the table to the back of the room, and the next day the hotel put a heavy auxiliary hood across the top of the window, around the regular blackout curtains. There have been no more complaints.

London decided to keep daylight-saving time all winter. That puts us six hours ahead of New York, and eight hours ahead of Denver. It seems a little odd to think, when getting up in the morning, that in Albuquerque it is the night before and my friends there are just going to bed (or at least should be if they're leading a clean, righteous life like me).

Everybody has read thousands of words about the blackout, but you cannot know what it's like unless you've been in it.

There is a slight reflected glow on the streets from the lights of automobiles and buses, when any of these happen to be passing. But if no such vehicle is near, you simply have to feel your way with your feet.

When I pull my curtains and open the window before going to bed, and look out upon London, I can see no more than if I were standing in the middle of the Sahara Desert on the darkest night of the year, blindfolded and with my eyes shut. Looking down from my sixth-story window, I can't see a single pin point of light anywhere.

The curbs in London are painted white, which makes walking a little easier. All light poles and safety-zone posts are painted black with white rings. The fenders of cars used at night are tipped with white. All moving vehicles carry lights, but they are mere pin points.

Pedestrians are permitted to use flashlights — called "torches" here — provided these are small, or shaded, and aren't pointed upward. I had been told back home that torches and batteries could no longer be bought in London, but they can. The price of batteries has been fixed by the government at a maximum of twelve cents.

Traffic lights are hooded from above, and the glass itself is painted a solid black except for a little cross in the middle. This is the tiniest of slits, yet from two or three blocks away it looks like a full green or red light.

People no longer motion for a taxi at night — it would be no use. They just stand on the curb and yell. At midnight, if I lean out of my window I can see no more than if I were blind, but I can hear people all up and down the street yelling for taxis at the top of their lungs.

It's miraculous the way taxis get about at night. When you get into one the driver clips off at twenty-five miles an hour and just keeps on going, ramming forward into nothingness.

I have achieved a new high in something or other for myself. The other night I found the correct bus in the dark, rode three miles into the night, felt my way across a street into a strange apartment house and got clear up to the apartment of a friend of mine. It made me feel so wonderful I took a taxi home.

PART IV: THE HEROES ARE ALL THE PEOPLE

1. ITS ALL TRUE

London,
January, 1941.

You have all read about London's amazing ability to take it, and about the almost annoying calm of Englishmen in the face of Hitler's bombs. Well, I am not going to dwell on this, since it has been much written about already. But I just want to confirm that what you have read in this connection is all true. I got it the very minute I stepped off the plane from Lisbon, and I've been getting it ever since.

You get it in the attitude of people, you get it in the casual way common folks talk, you get it just by looking around and seeing people going about their business.

The day before Christmas a hotel maid said, "I'll never forgive that old Hitler if he gives us a blitz on Christmas Day." That's typical British conversation. The attitude of the people is not one of bravado. It is no self-injection of "Do or die for dear old Siwash." It isn't flag-waving, or our own sometimes silly brand of patriotism. In fact, I've never seen or heard the word patriotism since coming here.

No, it is none of these. It is simply a quaint old British idea that nobody is going to push them around with any lasting success.

There are millions of people in this world who fear that England may eventually lose this war. Such an ending is inconceivable to the British.

The whole spirit of this war is different from that of the first World War. Over here there doesn't seem to be the pumped-up, hysterical hatred that we had for Germany in the World War. I've heard Germans referred to as "the Boche" only once in London.

You don't hear atrocity stories told around here about the Germans. You don't hear people making outlandish remarks. You no longer hear stories about Hitler being insane and a pervert. In fact, I've heard him referred to several times as a mighty smart man who has made very few mistakes. This isn't spoken sympathetically, or by pro-Nazis, but by common Englishmen willing to give the devil his due.

They say Hitler has made only one big mistake so far, and that was by starting the war in the first place.

And the spirit of bravery in the face of death is different in this war too. You all remember, or at least have read about, the eat-drink-and-be-merry-for-tomorrow-we-die spirit of soldiers on leave in the first World War. It was fatalistic, and dramatic, and what-the-hell. It was champagne and girls and on with the dance while there's still time.

That's not true in this war. There is night life in London, but not that daredevil kind of night life. People dance quietly. Late parties are rare. Drunkenness is not common. Soldiers on leave act much like civilians in peacetime. For in this war it isn't the soldiers who may

When the King goes out to inspect his heroes, they aren't long lines of straight-standing men in khaki with polished buttons. They are grimy firemen and wardens in blue overalls, so tired they can't even stand up straight for the King.

When just ordinary people at home may die tomorrow, heroics go out the window.

People aren't filled with a madly sweet compulsion to crowd a lifetime of fun into their few remaining hours. No, they are too busy, too poor, too tired, and too placidly determined to win by sticking it out.

It's a funny war. As someone remarked, the front-line trenches are four miles straight up above London, and the heroes are all the people.

It is true that all eyes in England look toward America.

My American accent alone is a key to unlock almost any door in London — except the doors of the extreme upper classes, of course.

And just as American public opinion about the war changes gradually, so I believe the British feeling about the possibility of our entering the war is changing. A few months ago, they say, all England was rabid for America to come in. But now many people are looking beyond the mere emotional effect of our entrance. Many feel that if we came in, all our production would be kept at home and England would get less than she is getting now. About a third of the people I've discussed the matter with feel that way. But almost without exception they do feel that we should furnish cargo ships and convoy them with our warships.

Today every London conversation eventually switches around to "He's up to something. What do you think it is?" Nine times out of ten Hitler is referred to as "he" rather than by name. Even the newspapers do it sometimes.

Something is being cooked up — everybody is sure of that. Most people think he will attempt an invasion before spring. Many think he will unwind an aerial blitz over London this month that will make the September bombings seem tame.

Any night he may start it. Any night people expect it. And they are ready. They feel that Hitler has not got anything that they, the ordinary people, can't take.

And after being here with them for a few weeks I believe they are right.

2. THE CUPBOARD'S NOT BARE

London,
January, 1941.

Food isn't a very romantic subject. You've never heard of a medal being presented to a war hero because he lived on one meal a day. The girls don't flock around the English farmer who makes two potatoes grow where only one grew before. But believe me, food in this war is only a jump or two behind planes and big guns in importance.

And as each month passes, the food problem will become increasingly vital to both sides. Ultimately, perhaps years from now, it may be that food will decide who is to win this war.

It is too early yet for any food shortage to begin making deep marks on the warring populations. They say food is still plentiful in Germany, and I know that England is in good shape. That is obvious to anybody who just eats around.

There is rationing, of course. Prices are high, and some things are so scarce they have almost ceased to exist. But as to the basic things that are needed to keep body and soul together, the situation in London hasn't reached even dead seriousness.

"Dispersal" is becoming more and more the theme of England in wartime — dispersal of troops, of factories, of children, of food. The bombings have brought that about. Scatter every vital thing all over England in tiny units and small groups — that's the keynote. Today only 80,000 of London's one million children are left in the city. They are all over England.

They tell me that the soldiers, with some exceptions, eat and sleep in groups no larger than thirty. Army trucks are always parked a good fifty yards apart so a single bomb won't get more than one of them. Factories have branches everywhere. And as for food, it is stored in thousands of nooks and crannies all over Great Britain.

There are stocks of food in empty garages, in old meeting halls, in unused theaters, police stations, barns, cellars. No one-night blitz, no matter how terrific, is going to wipe out any notable portion of Britain's stored food.

And speaking of dispersal, the Ministry of Food keeps only a skeleton staff of 250 in London. The bulk of the ministry's staff of about 2500 are in the country.

England began working out a wartime food-control plan four years before the war started. It even had all the ration books printed and waiting months before the war.

The first rationing was not put into effect until four months after the war started — that is, in January, 1940. Bacon, butter and sugar were the first items dealt with.

When a certain food is rationed, that does not necessarily mean the country is running short of it. It means that the government considers this particular food to be essential, and so it begins rationing to conserve a surplus for the far future. Also, many things are rationed to insure an equal distribution — so the rich people won't eat up all the things the poor couldn't afford if there were no such controls.

Today in England it is almost impossible to get onions, raisins, eggs, lemons or cheeses. Yet none of these things is rationed, because the government considers them nonessential to sturdy, healthy living. It is ready to let them go out of existence for the duration.

Today rationing applies to the following items in the following ways:

BACON AND HAM — Four ounces a week per person. (Peacetime consumption averaged 5.6 ounces.)

BUTTER — Two ounces of butter and four ounces of margarine a week. (Before the war, people averaged 7 ounces of butter.)

SUGAR — Eight ounces a week. (Consumption has been cut more than half; it used to be 17 ounces on the average.)

TEA — Two ounces. (Prewar consumption was 2.9 ounces.) But tea is not really short in England, as you can get it in any restaurant and nearly every grocery. Consumption is down only about one-fourth.

MEAT — The rationing of meat is based on price rather than on weight, because of the many qualities available. People today are allowed to buy one shilling tenpence — about 37 cents — worth of meat per person per week. This means about two pounds of fair beef. Fowl is not rationed, and there is a good supply.

As an example of how rapidly things change, since I wrote the above, two days ago, the weekly meat allowance has dropped to 30 cents' worth; and pork liver, kidney, heart and sweetbreads have been added to the rationed list.

The government makes mistakes that cause some confusion, as all governments do. For example, in dealing with rabbits the government set a maximum price for the retailers but none for wholesalers. As a result, the grocerymen must pay 17 cents a pound for rabbits but they dare not charge their customers more than 15 cents. The upshot is that plenty of rabbits are wasting away in warehouses.

The cut in sugar is probably what pains the average Englishman most. The English people have been used to tremendous quantities of sugar, probably a great deal more than was good for them. Doctors think this cutting of sugar consumption in half will be a fine thing for the national blood pressure.

The stores are nearly sold out of candy. I went to one today which had just one box of candy left. Chocolates run from 50 cents to $1 a pound, and they're not very good either. Many of the pieces are filled with dry cake.

When you eat in restaurants, the finest places give you two small cubes of sugar with each cup of coffee; the medium-priced and cheap places only one. And I don't like coffee with one cube of sugar.

Back in Lisbon I kept slipping cubes of sugar into my pocket from the hotel table, and I arrived here with about twenty. So for a while I had an extra one to drop in each cup of coffee, but they're all gone now. If I were making this trip over again I would throw away my shirts and bring three pounds of sugar.

There are approximately forty-six million people in the United Kingdom, so England prints fifty million of her food ration books. For everybody must have one. In the past, new books have been mailed out every six months. Starting in July, 1941, the books will be good for one year. Also, instead of tearing out coupons, the grocer will merely cancel them with a stamp.

People the world over love to figure out stupendous statistics, and the Food Ministry is no exception. It has estimated that these changes will save a thousand tons of paper and will dispense with the handling of 14,500,000,000 coupons a year.

Each member of a family, including each child, gets a ration book. Then the housewife goes to her favorite grocer and registers. She isn't allowed to change grocers except at six-month intervals, unless she moves. And she can trade only where she is registered.

Although I carry a ration book I couldn't buy anything on it unless I first registered at a store. Even then, if I wanted something scarce, such as oranges, eggs or onions, they wouldn't sell me any because of my not being an old customer.

Rationing is a complex affair. If you eat at home you can buy only so much a week. Yet you can go to a restaurant and get all you want, without even showing your ration book.

The hotels do their buying in big lots and can get choice things, but they, too, are rationed. Today they are allowed only 50 per cent of the bacon and ham they used last May. In January, 1941, they are getting less than half the meat they used in January, 1940; and now that is being cut still further.

They are allowed to give each diner only one-fourth of an ounce of butter and margarine (only one-twelfth of an ounce of this can be real butter), and they will serve you only one meat course.

If you live in a hotel you can stay for five days without a ration book. After that, they take the coupons from the book at the end of each week.

You can eat in public places for practically any price you care to pay. At our hotel it runs around two dollars for dinner, so I eat elsewhere. Dinner at Simpson's, with soup and dessert, will cost better than a dollar and a half, yet the other night at one of Lyons' numerous "Corner Houses" we had a good enough dinner, with music and everything, for 50 cents. The place was packed with soldiers and their girls, and I don't mean officers.

Only the more expensive places give you napkins now. At night, eating places are rather infrequent, so you almost have to eat at whatever place is handy.

You hardly ever see real butter in the restaurants. They serve margarine instead. At the Food Ministry it's pronounced with a hard "g," as in Margaret. It's all right, too. The government now requires that all margarine be injected with vitamins "A" and "D," and they say it has all the food qualities of real butter.

Also, you never see real cream. What you get is a ghostly white mixture of vegetable oils. It's thicker than cream and it has the oily texture of mayonnaise, but I can swear that it isn't bad at all.

As cargo space in English ships grows more and more precious, the importation of foods is increasingly restricted. Anything bulky is cut out. They have now stopped importing any fruit whatever, except oranges. Even canned fruits have been stopped. To take the place of fruit in diets, the government is encouraging Englishmen to eat more vegetables and grow more vegetables.

Most food prices in England are controlled by the government, but even so the average cost of food has gone up 22 per cent since the war started. As in all inflations, either in wartime or peacetime, wages have not risen accordingly. Hence many people have a tough time making both ends meet.

I will give you a list of representative food prices. Some of them do not seem so extraordinarily high, but you must remember that the average white-collar employee in England doesn't make as much as we do at home. Also, he pays out more in taxes.

Bacon is 35 cents a pound, in our money. The best butter is 35 cents, with the average quality 32 cents, but you don't get a pound a week unless there are eight in your family. Margarine comes in two grades, at 9 cents and 15 cents. Sugar runs around 7 1/2 cents a pound, tea 50 cents, and joint steak costs about 42 cents a pound (when you can get it). Stewing beef is around 30 cents, and joint roast about 36 cents a pound.

In meats you take whatever the dealers happen to have. Often you have to accept mutton instead of beef. There is no pork at all. The price of turkeys for Christmas was controlled at 50 cents a pound; whereupon chickens, which were not controlled, shot up to 60 cents a pound.

Eggs are 80 cents a dozen, but you can get only about four eggs a week at the stores. Oranges are 3 cents apiece and are still obtainable, although they are growing scarcer. You can get lemons and onions only when a new shipment arrives, and they won't be arriving much longer. Lemons are 11 cents a pound. Apples have been up to 35 cents a pound, which is three or four apples; but the price is now controlled at 20 cents a pound for the very best, running down to 11 cents. Soon there will be no more apples, until England's own crop comes in next fall. Some grapefruit have been coming from the Bahamas and Palestine; they run from 10 to 20 cents apiece.

Bread stands at about 14 cents for a four-pound loaf, and there is plenty of flour. The government subsidizes the bread makers, for it wants everybody to be able to buy bread cheaply. Bread will be one of the last items ever to run short.

First-grade potatoes average 18 cents for seven pounds. Milk is 7 1/2 cents a pint, but for children under five and nursing mothers it is cents. And all families with incomes of less than $8 a week can get milk free. Some three million people are eligible for this free milk, and two and one-half million of them are taking it.

The English feel deeply the present shortage of "biscuits" or, as we would call them, sweet crackers. These biscuits are of many forms, candied and filled, and the English people practically lived on them, along with their tea. But they have almost gone out of existence.

Whenever a shipment of precious things comes in they are ladled out by the grocer as great favors to his best customers.

An American friend of mine read in the papers about a new shipment of onions, so she asked her grocer if he had any. He said he didn't have a one. But then he disappeared into a back room for a moment, and when he returned he slyly handed her a sack and said, "Here are your oranges. Madam." When she got home she found two wonderful onions in the sack.

Most of my eating has been done in hotel dining rooms. They are packed at night with wealthy-looking Englishmen and women. Almost daily I hear some Englishman express a little shame at sitting there eating such a fine meal, and a little revulsion at the sight of hundreds of well-fed diners like himself around him, when so much of England's population can't eat that way.

As for myself, I have ham and eggs every morning for breakfast, where I had expected none at all. I couldn't have this if I weren't "eating out"; and I, like the Englishmen who eat at hotels, feel a little guilt at each mouthful I take.

With Germany bearing down harder in her U-boat strangulation campaign, there is more talk in the newspapers and among groups about stricter regulation of food. The striking thing about this talk — and I think it is an example of British character — is that the people want the Food Ministry to cut down on food faster than it is doing.

You can hardly conceive of the determination of the people of England to win this war. They are ready for anything. They are ready to take further rationing cuts. They are ready to eat in groups at communal kitchens. Even the rich would quit their swanky dining rooms without much grumbling.

If England loses this war it won't be because people aren't willing — and even ahead of the government in their eagerness — to assume a life of all-out sacrifice.

3. STREET SCENE

London,
January, 1941.

Along the nearly two miles of Regent and Oxford Streets where the big stores and fashionable shops are situated, I believe the windows have been blown out of two-thirds of the buildings. But the store owners have been ingenious about fixing up the damage.

They cover the great gaping front of a shop with wallboard, leaving a rectangular opening about the size of a table top right in the center. They put a pane of glass across this opening, and then they install a window display just as before, except on a smaller scale. Often the wallboard front is painted blue or brown or gray. Some of the stores even have hunting scenes or marching soldiers painted like a frieze across the top of the new wallboard front.

The result of all this is that instead of looking like patchwork, it makes what seems to me a neater and more attractive line of store fronts than before the bombings.

When a building is only slightly damaged by a bomb it is immediately repaired. Workmen are busy day and night cleaning out rubble and putting buildings together again. It is amazing how quickly they can turn a scene of destruction back into something normal.

But if a building has been too badly damaged for repair it simply stays that way until the war is over. No rebuilding from the ground up is permitted. The government needs all materials too badly — cement, bricks, steel. As a result, when the war is over England will probably have the greatest building boom in the history of the world. And maybe this very boom will be the thing to hold down unemployment and to ease the terrible shock of nonproduction and depression that follows all wars in all countries.

Maybe that will be one of England's silver linings.

The most puzzling thing to me about all the work of repairing and shoring up buildings and erecting shelters is where all the brick comes from. There are so many hundreds of surface shelters, so many thousands of bricked-up windows and protective walls, so much buttressing and fortifying and repairing, that you'd think there couldn't have been that many bricks in the world. Yet you see more bricks stacked up everywhere, in alleys, along sidewalks, even in lobbies of buildings, ready for use. And these are all new, whole bricks.

Don't tell me the British don't have a sense of humor.

I never get tired of walking around reading the signs put up by stores that have had their windows blown out. My favorite one is at a bookstore, the front of which has been blasted clear out. The store is still doing business, and its sign says, "More Open than Usual."

A sign on a barber shops says, "Blown Over Here from Across the Street." A sign on a bomb-scarred pub says, "Even Hitler Can't Stop Us from Selling Watney's Ale." And in front of a beauty shop along the Strand there is a sign saying, "Non-Stop Perming During Raids."

The other day I noticed a piece of stone about the size of a walnut lying under the radiator in my room. I picked it up and examined it. It was rounded at one end, and you could tell from the other end that it had been freshly broken off something. I studied it a long time, and finally came to the conclusion that it was a toe off some statue, or possibly from the sculptured frieze that adorns the roofline of our hotel. But how did it get into my room?

It suddenly dawned on me. And when the maid came in to straighten up I said, "Maid, have the windows ever been blown out of this room?"

"Why, yes," she said; "just a few days before you came. But they put them back in, you know."

They did a nice job of clearing up my room, but they forgot to look under the radiator. So I have a souvenir.

And now at last I am all equipped with a steel helmet and a gas mask. A friend who has just left for America gave me his. As soon as he was gone I brought the mask up to my room and tried it on. It is a big one, issued by the American Embassy, and it is so complicated that I can't make head nor tail of it. If the gas ever comes I might as well throw this contraption out the window and take a deep breath.

The famous fore-and-aft hat of the London bobby is gone for the duration. Today all policemen wear steel helmets. These are painted dark blue, with "Police" in white letters on the front.

London is fairly crawling with policemen. You meet half a dozen in every block. I understand there are now 40,000 bobbies — just double what there used to be. They are mostly young and soldierly looking, and I have found that instead of being austere they are very friendly. In fact, they will talk your head off if you stop to inquire your way.

London is plastered with posters and signs of warning, instruction and advice. Many of them are illustrated. For instance, one of them pictures a man and a woman gawking skyward, and the inscription says: "Don't stand and stare at the sky when you hear a plane." Then it explains that planes drop their bombs long before they are over the objective, and warns that if you stop to look up when you hear motors you may get one smack in the face.

A few blocks from my hotel is a huge store called His Majesty's Stationery Office. There you can buy for a few cents any one of thousands of detailed booklets on war-time food, arms, shipping, air raids, bombs, and so on, which the government has issued.

There is always a crowd in front of the counters, buying wartime education.

Many automobiles have little printed signs on the windshields saying, "Free lifts at your own risk." These are driven by suburbanites who get extra rations of gasoline for bringing other people to work. There are 20,000 of these now, but the arrangement is likely to be discontinued, for public transportation is practically back to normal.

Newspaper cartoonists are having a lot of fun with these small details of wartime life. For example, just after the British captured Bardia in Libya, a Daily Express cartoon showed Mussolini standing alone in the desert thumbing for a ride, and Hitler flying over in a German plane with a sign on it saying, "Free lifts at your own risk."

Nearly all the stores and offices close at four o'clock so people can get home before the blackout. At four-thirty the sidewalks and streets resemble Broadway. At five-thirty they look like Main Street on a dull Monday night.

Since gasoline is rationed, I was astonished by the heavy daytime traffic. There is constantly a solid wall of those big red double-decker buses, and there are so many private cars that I don't see how the streets could hold any more. I hate to think what traffic was like in peacetime.

A friend of mine says he thinks the autos here must run on air. People get only a couple of quarts of gas at a time. When you get into a car the gas needle always seems to register zero, but somehow they keep on running.

I've just had my first air-mail letter from the United States. It was eighteen days on the way, which I'm told is faster than usual. Many air-mail letters take a month. American magazines and newspapers do not arrive until six weeks after their appearance back home.

I remember reading that in September it took five days for a letter to be delivered right here in London, but now I get mail in the morning that was posted the evening before. The local postal service seems to be completely normal.

London's weather is not so bad as I had always heard, at least not yet. Incidentally, the censors won't let you cable anything about the current weather — what it is like this morning, for instance. That might give the Germans an idea.

Newsboys in the streets of London never open their mouths. I wish our newsboys would develop that habit. Over here they just write the biggest news of the day on small blackboards with chalk, or print it on white paper, and prop these bulletins on the building walls beside them. Most of the "newsboys," incidentally, are old men.

Taxi meters here start at the equivalent of fifteen cents. A trip costs about the same as, or perhaps less than, in New York. In the daytime there are plenty of taxis everywhere, and the taxis are a sight to behold. All of them look as though they had been designed in Queen's Victoria time and ought to be pulled by horses. But they run fine, and I swear they can turn around in their own length.

One of the few things I have found that are cheaper here than at home is a haircut. I paid only thirty cents the other day in the hotel barbershop, and since then I've seen haircuts advertised at fifteen cents. I'm going to get a haircut every day from now on — enough to last me for a year or two.

4. THIS IS THE WAY OF WAPPING

London,
January, 1941.

This is the way the people of London are.

Last night I was standing in the dimly lighted office of the marshal of a big air-raid shelter in the East End. A bareheaded man with a mustache, a muffler and a heavy overcoat was sitting in a chair tilted against the wall. I hadn't noticed him until he spoke.

"Have you been around Wapping?" he asked.

Wapping is a poor, crime-heavy, conglomerate, notorious section of London. Also it has been terrifically bombed, as has all of London's waterfront.

"No, I haven't," I said, "but it's one place I'd like to see."

"Well," said the man, "I'm a policeman and tomorrow's my day off. I'd like nothing better than to show you around Wapping if you would care for me to."

Would I care for it! To get around Wapping with a policeman as a private guide — you can't beat that if you're out to see London. I jumped at the chance.

So Mr. Ian Rubin, London bobby, and I walked six miles around Wapping. We did back alleys and dark places, burned warehouses and wrecked churches, block after block of empty flats. We did Wapping with a fine toothcomb. And so I'm in a position to say that as far as Wapping is concerned there almost isn't any Wapping any more.

Wapping is one part of the big borough of Stepney. Today its population is a mere few hundred. The entire ward was compulsorily evacuated in that first awful week of the blitz. They put people on boats and took them down the Thames. Those who have come back are mostly men.

In normal times Wapping would be a swarming, noisy mass of humanity, a population as dense as in our Lower East Side in New York. Today I walked block after block and met only half a dozen people. There was no sound in the streets. The place was dead. It was like a graveyard.

We walked into the big inner courtyard of a square of tenement flats. Rear balconies on each floor formed the walls of a square. The windows were all out; the walls were cracked; abandoned household belongings lay where they had been thrown. In the balconies above, no faces peeped over the railings. There was no sound, no movement, no life in the whole block. It was the terrible silence of that Wapping courtyard that got me.

Policeman Rubin and I walked on. We went into the station of a demolition squad — the men who pull down dangerous walls before turning over the general job of demolition to others. These are brave men. Five of them, in workmen's clothes, were sitting before a crackling fireplace. There was nothing for them to do today — but there might be any time.

They were very friendly, but I could barely understand their Cockney speech. One of them asked me if it was possible to write a letter to San Francisco. One of his fellow workers answered for me. "Sure, you dummy," he said. "You can write anywhere you want."

Everyone of these men had been bombed out of his flat, one of them three times. Their wives have been evacuated, but they stayed on to work — a part of London's great civilian army.

We stood now in a vacant lot where until last September there had been a five-story block of flats. It was fully occupied when a bomb hit. On the wall of a building across the alley you can still see the handprints of a man who was blown from his flat and smashed to death against the wall.

We stood amid the wreckage of a church, in which Policeman Rubin himself had toiled all night helping to reach a mother superior who had been buried in the debris. She was dead when they found her.

We went to see the Church of St. John of Wapping, well known to American tourists. Only the steeple was left, and it was being torn down for safety's sake.

We passed a pub where in the old days pirates and smugglers used to gather from the ends of the world to sell their illicit goods. It has been boarded up since September.

We passed an undamaged warehouse, where big sacks of East Indian spice were being loaded onto drays, and the smell was sweet and wonderful.

We came to a street sign that said, "Danger. Unexploded Bomb." So we walked around it.

Policeman Rubin showed me where a time bomb fell at the edge of a school. They couldn't get it out, so it lay there nine days before blowing the school to smithereens. The wreckage of the school still lay there in a heap.

I saw firemen damping down the inside of a warehouse in which a small new blaze had sprung up after months of smoldering.

I saw great mounds of burned newsprint paper, and other mounds of scorched hemp. I saw half walls with great steel girders hanging, twisted by explosion and fire.

But I saw whole warehouses, too; for Hitler didn't get them all.

We wandered back and forth through dead, empty streets, and looked at hundreds of ground-floor apartments where rubble-covered furniture stood just as it had been left. The owners probably will never come back for it.

We walked for another hour, Policeman Rubin and I, and then suddenly we came upon a small store with the wallboard front and little show-window center which are today the badge of a bombed establishment that's still doing business. And when I saw that window it dawned on me that in a solid hour of walking this was the first open store window I had seen.

Every other doorway and window in an entire hour of walking through the heart of a city district was a door- way or a window into a room that no longer held human beings or goods.

That is the way in Wapping today.

There will have to be a new Wapping when this is all over.

5. THE PYNTED AWL

London,
January, 1941.

We got on a bus, a friend and myself, to see more of London's devastated East End, where the poor people live, London buses are double-deckers, and you can smoke on the top deck, so we sat up there.

You don't just pay a flat fare in London. The conductor comes around and sells you a ticket to wherever you want to go. But we weren't sure just where we wanted to go, not knowing London well.

"I think we'd like to go around the Isle of Dogs," I told the conductor. So he told us where to change buses.

While waiting for the second bus we bought four apples (thirty cents) and ate them. This second bus took us only a short way, and we had to get off and walk two blocks, for the street had been blown up. A big group of men in workmen's clothes stood waiting for the next bus.

"Is this where we get a bus to the Isle of Dogs?" we asked.

One little stoop-shouldered fellow with yellow teeth and a frazzled coat said, "Just where do you want to go?"

We said we didn't know. He laughed and said, "Well, this bus will take us there."

So we all got on, and after a while a big man who was with the little fellow moved back and said he and the little fellow were going to walk through a tunnel under the Thames and would we like to get off and go with them. We said, "Sure."

It was a foot tunnel, not big enough for cars. These two men work on barges carrying freight up and down the Thames. They leave home one morning and don't return until the next afternoon. They were carrying tin lunch boxes now.

The big fellow had been to New York six times, before the first World War, working on ships. He told us about it as we walked through the tunnel.

At the other end we came out into what is known as Greenwich. The two men walked us past Greenwich College, which is very old. We stopped before some iron gates and peered through them at some far domes.

"Now that there," said the little fellow, "that's the fymous pynted awl."

"The what?" I said.

"The pynted awl," he said. "You know, doncha, the fymous pynted awl — the pynted ceilin', you know."

And then I realized he was saying "painted hall." So we looked appreciatively.

"All American tourists knows it," he said. "The artist he lyed on his back in a 'ammock for twenty years pyntin' that ceilin', and when he got through he found a mistyke in it and he went cracked worryin' about it. Nobody else to this d'y has ever been ayble to find the mistyke. You tell the Americans the bombs heynt touched the pynted awl."

We came to the little fellow's corner, so we shook hands and said good-bye. The big fellow got on a double-decked trolley with us, and do you know that this cockney, a complete stranger, insisted on paying our fare — and him as poor as a church mouse! He said people had been nice to him in New York. But that was twenty-five years ago.

After a while we said good-bye to him and got on another bus. It took us down into Blackwall Tunnel, back under the Thames. Then we got out and walked down into the neighborhood of the great West India docks. They won't let you onto the docks, but we could peep through.

It was raining now and very cold, and it was getting dark. We walked amid wreckage and rubble and great buildings that stood, wounded and empty. It was ghostlike and fearsome in the wet dusk. Poor, pitiful East End! True, Londoners say the slums should have been knocked down long ago, but this is a grievous way to go about it.

We got lost, and a policeman showed us the way again. At last we took another bus back toward the city. At Aldgate East Station I got off to change to the underground, while my friend continued on the bus.

It was pitch black now. I decided to get a bite to eat. I made out, faintly, the form of a policeman, and asked him where I could find a place to eat. He said there was a pub around the corner, three doors away. I felt my way around, but couldn't find the door of the pub.

In a minute a figure stood beside me. It was the policeman. He pushed the door in the darkness but it didn't give.

"It's closed," he said. "But you can get something across the street, there where you see that little light behind the curtain."

So I felt my way across and into a tiny place. It wasn't very clean. There were bare tables, sawdust on the floor, and three candles burning on a counter.

"What kind of sandwiches have you got?" I asked.

"Hot or cold?" said the man behind the counter.

"Hot," I said. Whereupon he dished up a great big fried fish, filled the plate with crisp fried potatoes, and handed it over. I recognized the dish as the famous "fish and chips."

I wasn't too eager to eat it in such a place, but one bite was all I needed. I never tasted better fish or potatoes in my life. And my whole supper cost a shilling-twenty cents.

I got back to the underground and bought a ticket to Charing Cross, the station nearest my hotel. When I got to the station and came upstairs, ready to venture out into the complete blackness, I asked the station starter which direction I should take to walk toward the Strand.

All you have to do over here is open your mouth. In one word they know you're a stranger. And knowing that, they help you. The station man took my elbow, led me outside and across a couple of drives and sidewalks, and got me out into the middle of the street.

"Now go straight ahead," he said, "right up this street, and you'll come to the Strand."

He must have guided me for half a block. I made it to the Strand, and made it clear back to the hotel, which was about eight blocks. I didn't get lost, or run into anybody, or fall down. I walked into the Savoy feeling like King George himself.

PART V: GUNS AND BOMBERS

1. TEA, WITH SOUND EFFECTS

London,
January, 1941.

If I was going to get by with calling myself a war correspondent, I figured it was time to get out and see some shooting. So the War Office fixed me up with a solemn, complicated pass to spend a night with an antiaircraft gun crew. It took quite a while to arrange, but finally the day arrived.

I waited until late afternoon, then put on my galoshes and my tin hat, bought ten packs of cigarettes for the gun crew, got into a taxi and went off to the war. When I got there I found that instead of ten men there were hundreds.

A sentry took me to a little cabin where two officers were having tea. They wrote down the number of my pass, and said some boob had told them over the phone that my name was MacInernie. Then they asked me to have tea with them.

The day had been dark and gloomy, and the clouds were hanging low. I was disgusted, for my pass was only good for one night and it didn't look like flying weather to me.

"You can't tell a thing about it," one of the officers said. "Sometimes they come over on the most illogical nights."

Another officer, who was just going on twenty-four hours' leave, said: "They'll be over. They always come when I go on leave. It's never failed yet."

He left, and another officer came in and joined us at tea.

This hut was a sort of battlefront apartment. The officers don't live there, but they eat, sleep and work there, near the guns, while on duty.

A soldier in uniform poured our tea. As dusk came, he pulled down the blackout blinds. It was nearing six o'clock. The officers don't eat dinner until about nine-thirty, so they were having very late tea.

Now it was all dark outside. And suddenly the sirens went off.

We all looked at each other.

"I told you they might come," said an officer. But I could tell he was really surprised.

A telephone rang. The officer on duty listened for a minute and then pointed to a wall map, indicating a spot halfway between the Channel coast and London.

"They're right there now," he said. "They'll be here in ten minutes."

He leisurely finished his tea, and had started to put on his overcoat when the phone rang again.

"Righto," he said over the phone. And to us he said, "The men are running to the guns now. Come along, let's see what's up."

Each of the guns was set down in a sort of concrete cistern. These gun bases were built before the war started. One of the gunnery officers used to play on this very ground as a child.

There were several small rooms, entirely underground and heavily concreted. The instrument men sat down there, with headphones on, making red marks on a map of London. Each red mark indicated a plane. They'd erase the marks almost as fast as they put them down, and indicate new positions.

Up above, right at the center of this antiaircraft settlement, was a complicated instrument through which the artillerymen sight. In daytime they can get the exact bearings of a plane with this instrument, but at night it's no good. So they have to use a sound detector. This is a big revolving machine with phonograph horns, at which half a dozen soldiers sit in the dark and read illuminated instruments. It is extremely sensitive. The other night they got a Salvation Army band on it. Honestly.

One man calls out the readings by telephone to the control room below, where these are noted on charts.

I had got it into my head that these sound detectors were hooked directly to the guns and that the guns just automatically pointed and fired whenever the sound mechanism thought the time was propitious. But it isn't done that way. All the dope from the sound machine, and that which comes over the phone from other instruments all over London, is rapidly tabulated, and calculations are made, and the guns are then aimed and fired manually at wherever they figure the plane should be by that time.

The Germans were mighty busy this night. They were overhead constantly for four hours, starting fires and dropping heavy explosives, many of which we could hear blowing things to destruction around us.

"See!" said my friend the officer, standing there in the dark. "By all rights it should have been a quiet night, and now look at this! You were lucky."

Now we are standing down below, on the floor of a huge concrete "cistern" somewhere near London. It is a wet, chilly January night. A huge gun sticks its snout up out of the cistern against the faint light of a moon-tinted sky.

The base of the gun is half enclosed in a steel cabin, like the cab of a locomotive. On each side of the gun barrel sits a man on a stool, just like an engineer and fireman. The man on the right, by cranking a wheel, keeps the gun moving around on a swivel, following the hand on a dial which points toward the sound of motors in the sky. The man on the left similarly raises and lowers the gun barrel.

Down in the pit are other men. They are all in uniform, but here in the dark they are mere shapes. They might as well be woodcutters or farmers for all you can tell.

Nobody says anything.

Three men stand just behind and to one side of the gun. Before them, lying in a rack that moves with the gun, is a row of big shells. The shells taper down to a pencil-point end. That end is a steel cap, shiny bright, with figures and marks on it, and right in the end, like the eye of a needle, there is a small hole. One man stands there with a narrow steel punch stuck through this hole. He holds the punch in his right hand. In his left is a shielded flashlight pointing down onto the end of the shell so he can read those little figures which a few seconds later will be bursting through thousands of feet of sky. He stands there waiting — everybody is waiting—everybody is ready for the order.

Off in the darkness, some yards away, technical information is being relayed from one instrument man to another. The sound-detector boys phone, "One three five one four zero one four five," giving the course of the enemy plane. Over the phone from somewhere else in London comes the plane's altitude. Mathematicians figure the angle, the range, the bearing. They call out as they figure. It is all quiet, but it is tense and rapid. The officer in charge stands alone there in the darkness. He takes no part in the details. The enlisted men do all that.

Finally there is a shout: "Stand by to fire." The voice carries to all the gun crews, and each acknowledges with a yell.

We are about ready to shoot at a German. Let's go back to one of the gun pits.

The boys are waiting. Not a word is said. Then comes a yell: "One five." That's the order for setting the time fuse. When that yell comes it means that within a few seconds a shell will be on its way up into the sky.

It is a dramatic thing, like the opening gong of a prize fight, ending months of training.

At the yell, the man with the punch gives the tiny end of the shell a little twist. He has set it at "one five" — in other words, he has set it to explode fifteen seconds after leaving the gun.

It takes him less than a second. He steps back. The man next to him already has this huge shell in his arms. He half throws it into the arms of the man next to him. This one swings it onto a set of rollers and shoves it upward to the man on the left side of the gun cab. He jerks it off the rollers, switches it into a steel cradle alongside the gun barrel. A lever rolls the cradle over and the shell is in the gun. An automatic ram pushes it tight, the breech snaps shut and locks. It is all done in the dark.

The gun is ready. We all step back.

There is utter silence, absolute suspension of all motion. A newcomer puts his fingers to his ears and gets tense all over.

It seems like hours now that we have been waiting, although it is probably only a few seconds.

Then, faintly, out of the darkness and into your muffled ears comes a human voice, yelling "fire," and all the guns go off at once.

Your first experience in a gun pit is truly a shocking one.

From every side you seem to have been struck by a terrific blast of air that almost knocks you down. And somewhere around you — you don't quite place it — there are horrifying sheets of flame, as if everything on earth had caught fire and exploded. And mingled with both these things there is certainly the loudest noise you ever heard.

The whole thing shakes you, physically and spiritually. And before you have really come back to your senses, you are following the crashing shell on its journey. The terrible blast seems to go shattering and crashing its way on up, up into the heavens, with a series of great reverberations as though the climbing shells were bursting through sheet after sheet of waxed paper stretched tight across the sky.

And then, if you wait maybe half a minute, you can hear faintly the explosion of that very shell which a minute ago you saw being loaded into the gun. Now it is flying into a thousand vicious little pieces, miles up there in the darkness.

But by now the yell, "One seven," has come through the night, the dark shapes of boys in uniform have moved wordlessly in routine little motions there in the open-air cistern, and another shell is already tearing toward the moon.

Some people can't stand heavy gunfire at all. And I'll have to admit that the first four or five times the guns were fired during my night with the ack-acks I didn't like it either. I wished I was home in bed.

But then I swear I got used to it.

Our battery fired close to a hundred rounds that night. It got so we would stop talking a few seconds before the guns went off and then go on with the conversation as soon as the noise was over.

Some of the gunners were telling me about a photographer who came up one night to take pictures. On the first blast from the guns he started running blindly away and charged right into a wire fence, which knocked him down. But it was no disgrace, for people who are like that just can't help it.

The blast from these antiaircraft guns is almost beyond description, but I can give you some examples.

The door to one of the underground concrete rooms where the men doze during quiet periods had a brand-new steel latch. On my night with the battery, the first salvo broke that steel latch in two and blew the door open.

They use up light bulbs at a terrific rate. The concussion breaks the filament. In the soldiers' canteen only one light bulb was left out of the original six when I went down after an hour's firing. And in the hut where the officers on duty have their meals, the blast rocks the building, knocks dishes off the table, and puffs out the blackout curtains so that they have to be readjusted each time.

Rubber earplugs are available, but the men don't wear them. They get used to the blast, and it doesn't bother them.

An officer and I were standing in the dark listening to the Germans overhead.

"They sound as if they were flying along evenly," he said, "but they aren't. When there is a formation, they may be flying five hundred feet above and below one another. If there's just one, he flies a zigzag course. Not only that, but he goes up and down, too, like a roller-coaster. That's so we can't get a good sound gauge on him."

It always sounded to me as if there were only one plane in the sky at a time. But at the end of two hours I asked about it and the gunner officer said:

"It's hard to say, but I'd guess that anywhere from one to three hundred had been over tonight."

The value of antiaircraft guns is not measured necessarily by the number of planes they bring down — although the guns are officially credited with about 450 of the 3050 German planes shot down over

Britain since the war started. Their greater value is in keeping the raiders high and keeping them jumping around, which makes accurate bombing very nearly impossible. In fact, the average height at which those 450 planes were plugged from the ground was 16,000 feet.

Searchlights are almost never used any more. Consequently, the gunners can't see how near their shells are coming to the target. But they did have a fantastic sight a few nights ago. They were looking at the sky through binoculars when suddenly they saw, silhouetted against the moon, three German planes in formation. But before they could fire the formation was out of sight.

The boys say the Germans occasionally watch for gun flashes, then take a quick bearing and try to drop a bomb on the gun station.

Every morning the gun crews have drill. They can set the fuse, load and fire in a few seconds, but they get even better. And after the regular drills the boys practice voluntarily for hour after hour.

"Is that because they like guns," I asked, "or is it because they want to get ahead?"

"It's literally because they're that determined to win this war," the officer said.

This night with the antiaircraft gunners was my first glimpse into the soldiers' side of the war. I'll long remember one moment late in the evening when I stood between an officer and a sergeant there in the darkness with the guns roaring and bombs crunching and planes grinding overhead, and the British officer said:

"Isn't this ridiculous — all of us trying to kill each other? And we thought it would never happen again!"

2. MISCELLANY

London,
January, 1941.

The brother of a man I know has a hobby of riding around on a bicycle every morning looking for new bomb damage. He phoned this morning to report that he had a big special one. (Reports of unusual bomb damage are spread around town by mouth-to-mouth grapevine, since the newspapers aren't permitted to mention specific locations.) So we took a bus to the scene about two miles from our hotel.

The report was correct, plenty. We learned later that the damage was caused by a German plane which crashed with its full load of bombs. They found little pieces of the plane.

All the near-by houses had been blown down. Big stone buildings remained standing, but their office furniture was splintered and smashed into ruin. There wasn't a window left for six blocks in any direction. And yet a policeman said only a dozen people were hurt and nobody was killed. Many bomb explosions are as freakish as that.

All the public clocks in the area were stopped, but none at the same minute. Among the half dozen that I saw there was a variance of half an hour. The answer is that the blast moved the hands.

Some London buildings now have corrugated-steel shutters that are pulled down at night over windows and doors. They don't save the glass if a bomb hits close by, but they do prevent shattered glass from flying all around. In this particular explosion these steel shutters were bent and twisted, some of them bashed in but others ballooned out toward the street like a weak spot in an inner tube. That is another freakish thing about bomb explosions — the pull is often greater than the push.

I saw the statue of Peter Pan in Kensington Gardens today for the first time. I think it must be the loveliest statue in the world. There is a big bomb crater two hundred yards away, but the statue is untouched. I think they ought to remove it and bury it for the duration.

The statue of Queen Victoria at Kensington Palace has several small chips missing from the hem of the Queen's dress, the result of a small bomb that dropped a hundred yards away.

Many bomb craters in the parks are being filled with debris hauled from bombed buildings.

Three-fourths of the windows of Buckingham Palace are blown out and boarded up. In one window a torn, ragged blind has been hanging for weeks. I'll bet they wouldn't fix it for ten thousand pounds, for it shows all England that their King is taking it too.

While the checkrooms in restaurants will check tin hats and soldiers' rifles, they aren't supposed to accept gas masks, the point being to make you keep your mask with you all the time, just in case.

The streets are full of soldiers on leave, but you rarely see a sailor. There are so many different uniforms that I haven't got them all straight. But I can tell all the dominion soldiers, for they have the name of their country—Canada or Australia or New Zealand — spelled out on their shoulder tabs. And that is true also of foreign units in the British Army. You very frequently see the word Poland or Czechoslovakia or Belgium on officers' shoulder tabs.

The Poles, incidentally, have been doing some wonderful fighting with the British, especially in the air. They are highly skilled fliers, and they fight with a terrible zeal. England looks upon the Polish airman's uniform with deep respect.

The uniform of the Royal Air Force is a pale blue. England idolizes the R.A.F., as well it should. The uniform commands a deep-down gratitude the minute it is seen, whether on a wing commander or a corporal mechanic.

Another thing about soldiers on leave in this war — almost any place you go you can see a private and a colonel and their two girls eating together. No, it doesn't mean that the war has brought true social democracy to England. It merely means that conscription makes officers of some aristocrats and privates of other aristocrats, and when they're on leave they're both still aristocrats, regardless of their uniforms.

King Zog of Albania lives at a prominent hotel, and since he doesn't like to sleep in the hotel's regular shelter he sleeps in the basement dining room. The waiters have to clear out all diners shortly before midnight so the King can go to bed.

Bombs or no bombs, you can still see plenty of movies in London. You can also go to a play, or a ballet. You can play the dog races. You can watch prize fights. You can ice-skate at public rinks. You can sit and drink intoxicating spirits.

The government has just promised that there will be no rationing of beer, and although I wouldn't know personally, of course, my gumshoe men report that whisky is readily obtainable. Wines are getting short.

A few of London's movie theaters have been bombed out of existence, and most of the legitimate theaters are closed, with signs saying "Due to Present Conditions…" Yet several new plays have opened in the last six weeks. Pantomimes are showing as usual. There are concerts by the London Philharmonic, and the Anglo-Polish Ballet goes on twice a day. A new idea is the "luncheon ballet," which is becoming extremely popular. There are two of them, already. And there is also "luncheon Shakespeare."

All this daytime stuff, of course, is the result of the nighttime blackout and the German raids at night. With three or four exceptions, the movie theaters are open only in the daytime. The movies start as early as 10 A.M., and the last showing is usually around 5:30.

"The Great Dictator" is running at three theaters. You can also see "They Knew What They Wanted," "Northwest Mounted Police," "Strike Up the Band," "The Thief of Bagdad," "All This and Heaven Too" and "The Return of Frank James." This last one starts its last show as late as seven o'clock. I suppose that's because Frank is a tough guy.

Despite the winter weather there are plenty of open-fronted places called sports gardens, which are packed with pinball and claw machines. There is always a crowd playing them.

You have no trouble getting enough sleep these winter nights. The Germans come over every night the weather is fit, but it gets really noisy only a couple of nights a week. Even then it seldom lasts more than two hours.

Britain manufactured millions of rubber earplugs when the raiding was so bad last September and people couldn't sleep. But the public didn't take to them. They're uncomfortable, and anyhow people like to hear what's going on. At an Air Raid Precautions post the other night they dragged out a three-gallon can full of these little plugs, which look something like golf tees. The warden wanted me to take a quart of them. I didn't want any, but I took a handful to bring home as souvenirs.

War has given the English language some new words. At least, it has made some obscure words commonplace — for instance, "stirrup pump." That word is as common today as automobile or cigarette.

A stirrup pump is a small hand pump with its complement of a few feet of hose and a couple of buckets of water, for putting out incendiary bombs and small fires. They are scattered all over London — thousands of them — and everybody is supposed to know how to use one.

Sand is also all over the place. Right here in the Strand there is a green sack of sand, resting on top of two bricks, leaning against every lamppost. This is so everybody will know where the sand is; if an incendiary bomb falls near you, you won't have to run around frantically looking for sand to throw on it.

Many buildings have sandbags stacked against their bases, but not many new ones are being put up. For they don't seem to serve much purpose. To make this early precaution look more sightly, and also to protect the bags from weathering, many places have boxed in their sandbags. So now there appears to be just a huge toolbox sitting there on the sidewalk up against the building.

People at home wonder about the censorship over here. Well, on the whole it is not so strict. I know some American correspondents who think it should be stricter than it is.

There are only a few general subjects that you're forbidden to mention — such as troop movements, the location of guns, and the location of any specific bombings until after a certain amount of time has elapsed. There are also other items, such as not giving current weather conditions or the routes of ships or planes, or cabling anything about a fire until it is out. (The rules were relaxed on London's big night of fire.)

The best thing about the press censorship here is that you always know just what is being cut out. The censor calls you on the telephone. And you can even argue with him. Of course you usually lose out, but imagine arguing with the censor in some countries!

As far as my stuff is concerned, the censors have up to now cut out a total of not more than six sentences, and these were nothing I particularly cared about.

They don't censor opinion. If you wanted to, you could say that you think England stinks, and it would go through. I think the censorship has allowed America to get a pretty honest picture of what has happened over here.

There are no skyscrapers in London. Like Washington, the city has a height limit for building, something like eleven stories. But spires and belfries and cathedral domes reach to great heights.

I can't think of a single really large modern building in London that has been wholly destroyed by bombs, unless the bombing was accompanied by fire.

I don't believe there is an aerial bomb in existence that could knock down the Empire State Building.

3. THE BEAVER

London,
January, 1941.

I always thought that a member of the peerage gave off a constant white light, like an incendiary bomb, and that if you got caught in this light you became weak all over, your tongue froze and you were sort of hypnotized. It had never occurred to me that an English lord, when you actually met one, would be a human being. But now I've met one, and I'm still shocked to realize that he spoke real words to me and that I spoke words back to him.

The great man in question is Lord Beaverbrook, the big newspaper owner. But right now he is much more than a newspaper owner — he's the man who is rolling out the planes with which Britain intends eventually to win this war.

Lord Beaverbrook is Minister of Aircraft Production. There wasn't any such ministry until last May. Airplanes weren't coming off the line fast enough to catch up with Germany. Everybody was trying, but everybody apparently was trying in all directions at once. So Mr. Churchill put his finger on Lord Beaverbrook and said, "You're it."

I doubt if Lord Beaverbrook knew any more about aircraft production at that moment than I did, but he did know how to get things done. He has the American sense for ignoring tradition, and an almost inspired zeal for accomplishment. He stepped into his new job with a bang and said, "No, we won't cut red tape; we'll just ignore it."

What he did, and how he did it, must still remain in the secret files, but you can draw your own conclusions — Britain has been getting very bold in the air of late. Daylight raids across the Channel have become a steady occurrence.

People close to Lord Beaverbrook have a tenacious affection and respect for him, but as a public figure he has collected his share of dead cats. The English public considers him a robber baron. The aristocracy regards him as a man in trade. Plenty of bricks are hurled at his present success. People say, "Yes, he succeeded, but he did it by ruthlessly robbing other ministries."

I don't know that Lord Beaverbrook ever answers these jibes, but if he wanted to he could say, "Well, you all said the production of planes was the most important thing in this war. If that's true, then what was wrong with taking things from other departments?"

Lord Beaverbrook likes a fight, and he doesn't especially care for applause. As one writer put it, he'd "rather be cleverly attacked than fulsomely praised." He likes to be in there swinging against odds. And he has a vitality, both mental and physical, that exhausts the people around him.

When he jumped into this thankless job last May he became a new man. His asthma disappeared. He worked from nine in the morning till three the next morning. Like Edison, he can exist on little sleep. And he had his whole staff going at a high pitch. He loved it.

But now his asthma has come back, and he doesn't keep the ridiculous hours he did at first. When I said to him, "I'll bet you love your job, don't you?" he smiled and said, "I'd like to be out of it."

It's my guess that Lord Beaverbrook has aircraft production ironed out so well that it no longer tests him, and he is becoming bored with it. To me, that's just as pertinent an indicator of his success as the new audacity of the R.A.F.

Lord Beaverbrook was born in Canada. Before he was thirty he had made a million dollars. Then he came to England to make his mark. He was elected to Parliament long ago, in 1910. During the first World War he was Minister of Information. He is the best-known newspaper figure in Britain. He has taken a big hand in politics, and now again he is doing a vital war job for England. And yet he still sort of considers himself a foreigner.

When I sat down across the desk from him, the first thing he said was, "Well, what do you think of them, aren't they wonderful?" He meant the British people and the way they are taking the war.

"I'm a foreigner here, you know," he said, "so I can see them as they can't see themselves. They're the greatest race on earth. Nobody else could have pulled themselves together like this. I doubt if we could have done it in Canada."

"Could we Americans have done it?" I asked.

"Well, yes," he said. "At least in the East they could have."

I damned well resented that, being an old Montana cowboy myself. But then I remembered I was in Whitehall and not on the Powder River; so, like the British, I pulled myself together and carried on.

A little knot of half a dozen or perhaps a dozen men will emerge at the end of this war as the great leaders who pulled England through. Most of them will be men who forgot politics for the duration, men who laid aside their skittishness and slashed out and did things. They will be men who kept pace with the

British national character, not those who were dragged along by it. Lord Beaverbrook, I have no doubt at all, will be one of this select group. And for that reason I want to tell you all the little things I know about him. He has already been written about a great deal in America, but it takes a lot of writing to make the public know a man, so I'll just add my share.

He is of medium height, stocky though not heavy. His shoulders push forward, and when he sits at a table he almost seems to crouch. His face is sallow, and it leaves the impression of being square rather than round. His mouth is big, his lips pursed. His black hair is thin on top, but on the back of his head it is thick and heavy, almost down to the collar line. He was dressed in black when I talked to him.

Lord Beaverbrook doesn't speak like an Englishman. He still speaks like a Canadian, which means like an American. He knows America intimately. His last trip over was made in October, 1939, just after the war started.

"You know my friend Dick Merrill, don't you?" I asked.

"I certainly do," he said. "He came down to the boat the last time I was in New York. I sent him a cable when his new baby was born. I have flown with him a lot."

Lord Beaverbrook used to have his own airplanes. He still occasionally flies about England, visiting aircraft factories, but he goes in government planes now.

He owns three big London newspapers — the Morning Express, the Evening Standard and the Sunday Express. You've probably heard of his modernistic black-glass Express Building in Fleet Street. Back home, every time I read about Fleet Street being bombed I wondered if Beaverbrook's glass house had been hit. It has not, although buildings a hundred feet away have burned. In October a bomb did go through the roof of the Standard Building, however.

Since taking on the aircraft job, Lord Beaverbrook has paid almost no attention to his newspapers. At the Standard they didn't hear from him for weeks, until one day he called up and said, "What do you mean by attacking the Presbyterians in my newspaper?" His father was a Presbyterian minister and he himself knows the Bible intimately. He almost always quotes from it in his speeches.

He is very much opposed to smoking. He used to play tennis avidly but has given it up. Almost his only relaxation now is the movies. He is a movie fiend, and has a projector at his country home. He's crazy about Marlene Dietrich. As one of his fellow workers said. Lord Beaverbrook probably thinks the greatest contribution America could make to Great Britain would be to send over more Dietrich films. They say he has seen "Destry Rides Again" nine times.

Lord Beaverbrook loves to hear people singing together. He sings himself — but, as somebody has said, he has more rhythm than tone. His favorite songs are "Little Joe" and "See What the Boys in the Back Room Will Have."

Around town Lord Beaverbrook is known as "The Beaver." At the aircraft office he is spoken of as "The Minister."

He is a great friend of Richard B. Bennett, former Prime Minister of Canada, and he has Bennett at the ministry with him.

During the week Lord Beaverbrook sleeps at night in a heavily walled room at one of his newspaper plants. Week-ends he goes to a place outside of town, but even so he drops in at his office on Sundays.

He has two sons and a daughter. Max, the elder son, is in the R.A.F.

Lord Beaverbrook's government office is a lovely one, in contrast to the dark Victorian offices that many British statesmen occupy. It looks out across a park and down upon the Thames. The office is a large one, with rugs and deep leather chairs. On a table at Beaverbrook's left are four telephones — three black ones and a green one. The green one is for intercabinet communication.

Outside the office is a large room where six secretaries, all men, work. The door between is always open. Secretaries and technicians have constant access to the Minister. They are in and out all the time.

It is usual for Beaverbrook to be talking to four or five people at once about different things. He is a colossal asker of questions. Before you sit down he has found out whether you smoke, drink, fight, swim or speak Esperanto. At least, that's what everybody says. But he must have figured I didn't know anything anyhow, for he didn't pump me much.

He seemed to me to be in complete repose. He didn't impart any feeling that he is the slashing dynamo he really is.

In personality Lord Beaverbrook runs the scale. He probably would have been a great actor. He has one act of intimate confidence, one of savage bullying, one of grave piety, one of profound and devastating gloom. At times when he walks into a cabinet meeting, they say, you can hardly keep from crying, he looks so tragic. But the chief characteristic of Lord Beaverbrook is probably his wit. He has a brilliant but left-handed humor. People who don't know him well are often unable to tell whether he's serious or joking.

That wit of his can on occasion be scalding. They say he likes people who can stand up to his barrages. He's not a man who has to be agreed with. And on the whole he doesn't care what the public thinks or says about him. He likes to fight, that's all.

In getting things done he is not unlike Churchill. And that is the way to win a war.

4. SHOP TALK WITH THE R.A.F.

An RAF. Bomber Station,
February, 1941.

Although I can't tell you where it is, or give people's names, I am spending a few days with the Royal Air Force. The place is not near London.

My pass for visiting this certain bomber station is good for two days. The weather is nice here, but bad on the Continent, so nightly flights have been called off. But I don't care; for what I prefer, anyway, is just to sit around as I used to do at home on bad weather days and do a lot of "hangar flying" — in other words, just talk. These R.A.F. pilots had never heard the expression "hangar flying," but they thought it very apt and have started using it, so I guess I have now given my share of American aid to Britain.

There are many pilots at this field, and I have come to know some of them very well indeed. The R.A.F. boys are just like any group of fine aviators at home. They're the cream of the crop, and swell guys, from station commander on down.

A visitor is not permitted to describe an R.A.F. station, but I can say this: My greatest surprise was at its close resemblance to a big Army Air Corps field in the peacetime United States. I had expected to find things tense and hectic, with secret hangars and everything camouflaged to look like something else. I had expected to find the whole place rather makeshift, for quick moving; and that everybody would be in overalls and like firemen, ready to jump into their boots and go at a second's notice. It isn't that way.

The officers have pleasant private rooms. The enlisted men live in big permanent brick barracks. In the officers' mess there is a great sunny lounge room with a huge fireplace. It resembles a country club more than a battle station. There is a game room, with billiard and ping-pong tables and a tiger rug on the floor. There is bar service, so that the pilots can have a friendly drink at lunch and dinner time. During the day they go about their normal duties, testing and checking aircraft, practicing formation flying, attending to the countless clerical desk tasks which are necessary in running a flying field.

Only in the early afternoon, when they gather around a big map-covered table in the "briefing room" to lay out plans for that night's flight, and again when they take off one by one on the long journey to the land of the enemy, and once more when they begin to drop down one by one out of the black skies, is there any warlike feeling about the place.

Well, there is one other thing you notice, too. As we sat around the great lounge before lunch, with many pilots in the room, I was struck by the scarred faces of some of the men. There weren't a lot of them

— half a dozen at most — but they were enough to prick the illusion that this was a peacetime flying field. Yet the boys say they have lost remarkably few bomber crews in the last bitter six months. Almost everybody shot down over Germany has managed to land by parachute and is now in a prison camp. Fatal crashes on home soil have been comparatively few.

I asked how they got weather information from the other side, and they said it was difficult but, with their own observations and certain information that does come through, they were able to forecast pretty accurately. I asked the station commander why some night, just for the hell of it, he didn't call up Berlin on the radio-telephone and ask how the weather was over there. He laughed, and said he believed he would; but of course he won't. I'll bet they'd be so flabbergasted the first time that they'd tell him.

The R.A.F. boys have a high regard for the flying ability of their foes, and a healthy respect for antiaircraft fire from the ground.

They don't worry about shell fragments hitting their bombs and exploding a whole plane in midair, for such a smack doesn't set bombs off. In fact, occasionally they can hear shrapnel striking the bombs slung beneath their planes, and that's a sound they are glad to hear, for it means that the thick steel walls of the bombs have kept the shrapnel from coming up through the fuselage and into the seat of the pilot's pants.

I asked one boy whether he ever had a funny little feeling in his stomach when he sent a bomb on its way downward, and he said, no, not actually, although sometimes he did indirectly when he got to thinking about it later, back home. But any regret is overcome by the thought of what the Germans did to Britain first.

Among the rumors we occasionally get back home is that German planes are being turned out with very few and very poor instruments. The R.A.F. boys say that is nonsense. German planes shot down over England are all fully equipped with instruments, and these boys say their workmanship is superb. The lads who have to face the music don't fool themselves, as we sometimes do at home.

An all-night flight to Germany or Italy in a bombing plane is a long and grueling task. And it's the sort of job you can't keep on doing night after night, as though you were going to work in a mill.

In the heavy days of the spring of 1940 bomber pilots were making as many as five trips a week, but now the average is less. When they have made a certain number of trips they are "posted" for other duties — which means a rest. It usually involves transfer to a training station as an instructor.

Although the boys are all disappointed when bad weather washes out any one night's operations, still I believe they are a little glad to have the rest when it comes. It takes some months to work up the number of trips necessary before a man is given a rest. This station has only one man so far who is back on night bombing duty after having been posted. He came back in less than the scheduled time — because at the training station he talked so much about his experiences he drove his fellow pilots almost crazy!

The funniest incident I have heard about at this station is about one of their bombers that got lost and finally landed in Germany, just after daylight. The fliers asked some German farmers where they were, and the farmers told them. They got back in the plane and flew safely home.

But they rarely get lost, for they are thoroughly skilled at instrument flying when they arrive for duty.

I have a friend — the best one I've made, and whom I'm going to see again in another part of the world — who was telling me about a crash he'd been in. We were riding in a car as he talked about it — he and I in the front seat. I asked him if this was his only accident. He said "Yes," and then reached around and said, "Where's some wood to knock on?" Three other pilots were riding in the back seat, and they yelled as if they had caught somebody stealing jam: "Jimmy's shooting a line! Jimmy's shooting a line! He must be, if he's looking for wood to knock on."

You hear that term, "shooting a line," more than any other expression around an R.A.F. field. The boys razz each other with it. They don't spare anybody, no matter what he's been through. Anyone who talks about anything he has done is accused of shooting a line. And since everybody talks, everybody is eventually accused. It's all good-natured.

They had one pilot, now transferred, who was a colossal line-shooter. He would come back from every trip with the most fantastic tales of his adventures. He never repeated himself, and he never had a dull story. The boys felt lonesome for weeks after he left.

At home we have only a few sergeant pilots in the Air Corps, but Britain has many of them. It is not unusual for a great British bomber to be captained by a sergeant, who all during the trip is in command over the commissioned officers who make up his crew.

The greatest discomfort the bomber crews have is the cold. They almost freeze to death. The planes are heated by hot air from the engines, yet so much cold wind gets in that they really suffer. They're now getting electrically heated boots and gloves, which will solve the problem.

Unlike our airline transports, a bomber has only one set of controls. The captain and the second pilot have to trade seats when they relieve each other. One of the boys told me how one night over northern Italy, when he was second pilot but was flying the plane at the time, the motors suddenly went dead. So he nosed the plane over into a dive, and while they were diving straight downward he and the captain changed seats. The motors caught again at 3000 feet and they came home safely.

And incidentally, you know how worried we get on an airplane when one motor goes out? Well, it is not unusual at all for these bombers to come all the way from Berlin on one engine.

These young fellows admit that they do get scared sometimes. Scared — yet on the whole they take it just as a matter of course.

Usually they circle over the objective for an hour or so, dodging antiaircraft fire and getting a good sight on the target. One officer told me that once when he was flying as a second pilot, and not at the controls, he actually went to sleep right over Berlin — slept in his seat for half an hour and didn't wake up till the captain yelled at him to work out a course for home.

I asked if they ever saw German night fighters in the air. Not often, they said, but they've all had instances. One of my pilot friends says he has ordered his tail-gunner never to fire if he sees a German plane flashing past in the night, for there is always a chance the German didn't see them. This friend has had half a dozen cases where a German fighter whizzed past so close there was almost a collision, but the enemy never saw them at all.

The five men who go out in a bomber take a lunch of chocolate, cakes and fruit and a thermos bottle of hot tea or coffee. One pilot said he opened his hot tea one night and found that it was frozen solid. Most of them aren't interested in lunch while flying. What they really look forward to is that hot breakfast when they get home, just before daylight. One officer whom I know, a tail-gunner, doesn't care much for sweets and he always brings his bar of chocolate back with him from Germany for his five-year-old daughter.

A pilot flies the same plane every trip. And he tries to keep the same flying and ground crews. On days when he is not scheduled to go out that night, he hangs around the plane getting it all fixed up just the way he wants it. He comes to think of that plane as almost belonging to him.

A man bent on a mission of death finds time to appreciate beauty, too. One of the boys said the most beautiful sight he had ever seen was the Alps on a clear moon-lit night. He had never seen them before. They were covered with snow, and their dark-shadowed sides gave the effect of a ghostly etching.

Another pilot looked down one night on his way home and there were stars right beneath him. He thought sure he had got bottom-side up, but it turned out he was seeing a reflection from the sky in the English Channel below.

Pilots have various slang terms for things. An automatic pilot is known as George. An airplane is a kite. And of course the Germans are always referred to as Jerry. It happens that I have a very close friend back in America named Jerry. I hope when I get home she doesn't try to bomb me. If she does, I suppose I'll just have to shoot her down.

PART VI: THE CAVE DWELLERS

1. ALL I COULD BEAR

London,
February, 1941.

This war has driven millions of people to burrow underground like moles. On an average, one-fourth of London's population has slept underground in the past six months.

On nights when the raids are bad, about half of London is below the surface. And in certain sections, such as the Borough of Stepney in the poor East End, with its population of a quarter of a million, they say that on bad nights ninety-nine per cent of the people are down below. It is a sorry life.

I have been in shelters night after night after night. I've been in about fifty of them in all, from the lowliest to the most luxurious, from vast stockyards of places that hold 14,000 people, on down to refined little underground homes buttressed like Gibraltar.

It is going to be hard to describe a shelter so that you can picture it; just as it would be hard to describe a ship to somebody who had never seen one. For there must be as many kinds of shelters under London as there are kinds of ships on the sea. But in general, sheltering falls into four classifications: (1) the tubes, which is to say the subways; (2) private shelters, under hotels and apartment houses; (3) vast public shelters in the basements of thousands of strong buildings, and (4) Anderson shelters — the artificial cave that the home owner builds in the backyard for his family alone.

I suppose that back home we have read more about life in the tubes than in any of the other shelters. Possibly that is because it is forbidden to name other big shelters, for fear of directing German bombs to them. Yet fewer people sleep in the tubes than in any of the three other types of shelter.

Here are some figures to show just how much of London can get under shelter at night, how much of it actually takes shelter, and where:

(The last figures comes from a shelter census taken throughout Greater London on a recent quiet night.)

Tubes: Capacity 178,000, Census 96,000.

Private group shelters: Capacity 930,000, Census 209,000.

Public Shelters: Capacity 1,323,000, Census 368,000.

Anderson shelters: Capacity 3,418,000, Census 1,271,000.

Total: Capacity 5,849,000, Census 1,944,000

Taking into account the evacuation, on which there are no definite figures, let us assume that the population of Greater London today is eight million. Then these figures mean that there are shelter accommodations for nearly three-fourths of the people, and that on quiet nights only one-fourth of the population uses them. On bad nights this figure doubles.

When I say that only a fourth of London is burrowing in these winter nights, don't get the idea that the other three-fourths are out around the town. Only a few thousand are. The rest are at home, behind their blackout curtains.

In the past few weeks bad weather has disrupted the raiders, and they have been over London on an average only four nights a week. And only about one night a week has there been really heavy raiding. People grow nonchalant about it, possibly too nonchalant. But just let London get two bad nights in a row and see what happens. You would see well over half of London diving for the basements.

Today, after six months of hiding from bombs, the shelter population has become pretty well settled. The same people go to the same shelters each night. They sleep in the same spots, either in bunks or on the floor. The Ministry of Health is installing bunks so fast there are now some 350,000, and before spring the number will probably pass a million.

There are all kinds of opinion about the people who live in shelters. Social workers think they're wonderful. Some people consider them cowards. As far as I can see, they have the same strengths and weaknesses that people in the mass have everywhere, in war or out. They are just people doing the best they can with a situation that is pretty bad.

The shelters do harbor some conscription dodgers and petty thieves, and a horde of young men who refuse to act as fire watchers or do much of anything else. They are weak characters. At home they would be drugstore cowboys; here they're called "tube Cuthberts."

When life has simmered down to the point where you have to choose between being bombed and living like swine on the floor of a dungeon, then life has indeed become pretty bleak. And this isn't just in London. All over England people are burrowing in shelters at night. Millions of them are living through these sixteen-hour winter nights like that — just down there waiting in a tube or a basement or a dugout.

There is no denying that it's better than being dead, but it's a hell of a way to live.

I got my first view of an underground shelter crowd at the big Liverpool Street tube station.

It was around eight o'clock on a raidless night. A policeman in the upper vestibule told us just to go down the escalator and take a look — as though it were a zoo. So we did.

Somehow I must have thought that there'd be nobody down there that night, or that if there were they'd be invisible or something, because I wasn't emotionally ready at all to see people lying around by the thousands on cold concrete.

In my first days in England I had seen terrible bomb damage. I had seen multitudinous preparations for war. I had talked with wounded soldiers. I had gone through London's great night of fire-bombing. I had listened for hours to the crack of guns and the crunch of bombs. And although I didn't especially know it at the time, none of these things went clear down deep inside and made me hurt.

It was not until I went down seventy feet into the bowels of the Liverpool Street tube and saw humanity sprawled there in childlike helplessness that my heart first jumped and my throat caught. I know I must have stopped suddenly and drawn back. I know I must have said to myself, "Oh my God!"

We hunted up the shelter marshal, and talked to him for a long time. He was immensely proud of his shelter, and I suppose he had a right to be, for they say it is paradise now compared to what it was in the beginning. He told us to take a walk through the shelter and then meet him at the back entrance.

This is a new section of the tunnel, not yet used by trains. The tube is narrower than most of New York's subway excavations, and it is elliptical in shape. It is walled with steel casing.

We walked to the far end, about an eighth of a mile, through one tube, and then back in the parallel tube. On benches on each side, as though sitting and lying on a long street-car seat, were the people, hundreds of them. And as we walked on they stretched into thousands. In addition, there was a row of sleeping forms on the wooden floor of the tube, stretched crosswise. Their bodies took up the whole space, so we had to watch closely when we put our feet down between the sleepers.

Many of these people were old — wretched and worn old people, people who had never known many of the good things of life and who were now winding up their days on this earth in desperate discomfort. They were the bundled-up, patched-up people with lined faces that we have seen sitting dumbly in waiting lines at our own relief offices at home.

There were children too, some asleep and some playing. There were youngsters in groups, laughing and talking and even singing. There were smart-alecks and there were quiet ones. There were hard-working people of middle age who had to rise at five o'clock and go to work. Some people sat knitting or playing cards or talking. But mostly they just sat. And though it was only eight o'clock, many of the old people were already asleep.

It was the old people who seemed so tragic. Think of yourself at seventy or eighty, full of pain and of the dim memories of a lifetime that has probably all been bleak. And then think of yourself traveling at dusk every night to a subway station, wrapping your ragged overcoat about your old shoulders and sitting on a wooden bench with your back against a curved steel wall. Sitting there all night, in nodding and fitful sleep. Think of that as your destiny — every night, every night from now on.

People looked up as we came along in our good clothes and our obviously American hats. I had a terrible feeling of guilt as I walked through there — the same feeling that I have had when going through penitentiaries, staring at the prisoners. I couldn't look people in the face; consequently I didn't see very much of the human visage that night, for I looked mostly at the floor. But I saw all I could bear. I saw enough.

Since that first night I have seen so much of it I no longer feel that way about the shelterers in mass. Repetition makes the unusual become commonplace. Enough of anything dulls the emotions. But I still think my first impression was a valid one. I still think it speaks the frightening poverty of character in this world more forcibly than do the bombs that cause it.

A bombed building looks like something you have seen before — it looks as though a hurricane had struck. But the sight of thousands of poor, opportunityless people lying in weird positions against cold steel, with all their clothes on, hunched up in blankets, lights shining in their eyes, breathing fetid air — lying there far underground like rabbits, not fighting, not even angry; just helpless, scourged, weakly waiting for the release of another dawn — that, I tell you, is life without redemption.

2. DOUBLE-X

London,
February, 1941.

I went into an East End shelter, beneath a railroad track, with a friend who supervises repair work on shelter buildings. This railroad runs through the city on a high grade, the top of which is heavily arched over with stone. At the street level, under the tracks, are large rooms. And here underneath the rumbling trains people sleep at night.

It was about 11 p.m. when we went into one of the rooms. It was dungeonlike and gloomy, with only a faint light, and very cold. About twenty people lay on the floor on mattresses, covered with quilts. Everyone was asleep, or so we thought.

My friend looked at the ceiling to see if recent work aimed at stopping the seepage of water had been finished. We didn't say anything, but suddenly from among the recumbent forms came a woman's voice:

"When are we going to get bunks — after the war's over?"

The voice was old, but it wasn't a complaining voice, or a bitter one. There was even a note of gaiety in it.

The remark opened up other sleepers, and many of them put in an oar. They lay on their backs and talked up to my friend about the discomforts of this miserable place.

There were old men and women with lined faces. There were middle-aged men who said nothing. There were children. And side by side lay two girls — beautiful girls in their twenties — with nets on their hair and cold cream on their faces. At Ohio State they would be popular coeds. Here they lay on their backs on concrete floors, looking up as we stood and talked for some fifteen minutes.

And then in the midst of this conversation I heard — if you'll excuse me — what seemed to be someone using the toilet. The room grew silent for a moment, and the sound was magnified.

I didn't believe it could be true — here in public before children and elders and two lovely modern girls you'd have been proud to take to the Ritz for dinner. It seemed impossible among civilized people. But it was true. The only toilet in that room was a public bucket.

Nobody laughed or blushed. This vulgar intimacy had become accepted as a way of life under the whip of war.

As we left, the old voice with the gaiety in it called to me and my friend: "We'll all be dead before you get this place fixed up, so you'd better leave a deposit on a wreath for me."

They were all laughing as we left.

Shelter Double-X is in the East End. I call it Double-X because I can't give its real name.

People feel sentimental about Double-X, they have been there so long. Some ten thousand people live there every night. It is one of the biggest shelters in London. It is so big it is like a state fair. It takes you hours to go through it.

Openings have been walled up, and shock walls have been built a few feet in front of the entrances. The great vaultlike space is divided into bays, each holding more than a hundred persons. Each bay is numbered, and each one has its own submarshals, selected by the people themselves.

At first, ten thousand people slept on the floor. But now bunks are going in.

Double-X has two big first-aid rooms, with Red Cross nurses in charge. It has canteens. It has a wagon refreshment stand, run by a Negro. It has one vast long promenade devoted to nothing but milling up and down on parade, just like the boardwalk at Atlantic City, except under cover.

Double-X is not modern and not too immaculate, but it has the saving grace of having become a social center. People like to be at Double-X because they have so much fun. It's full of young people, handsome young people, walking and talking and laughing. And it's cosmopolitan. There must be somebody there from every nation on earth.

Everything happens at Double-X, from births to deaths. Evening classes for adults are held. There is a library. There are romances. Multitudinous soldiers on leave go there to find girls. Double-X is a big, jolly city, all under one roof. Its inconveniences are overshadowed by its personality. It is a gigantic human omelet, fried in war.

Now to a private Anderson shelter.

This is a half-above-ground cellar, usually built in a backyard. As I have said before, there are thousands upon thousands of them in Britain — in the suburbs, the small towns and the country they hold more people than all other kinds of shelters put together.

Any person making less than $20 a week is supplied free with the material for an Anderson. Others must buy their own.

An Anderson shelter is formed of walls of sheet iron, heavily banked on the outside with dirt. A direct hit will demolish an Anderson, but it is good insurance against a nearby blast and flying debris. The other day I saw one standing quite unharmed not 15 feet from a bomb crater that was 20 feet across.

But four people are miserably cramped in an Anderson shelter. Often the owners have trouble with water seeping up through the floor. And it is a problem to heat them without suffocating.

At first the Andersons were considered wonderful, but now the government is threshing over a new policy of shoring up and fortifying one room in your house as a healthier and safer shelter.

The average Londoner who sleeps underground every night has done a lot of shopping around before settling down in a particular shelter for the duration. It is something like looking for a new apartment to rent. The choice is based on what looks safest, and on whether you like the crowd or not.

As horrible as shelter life seems to me, one marshal told me he felt sure that after the war many people would want to keep on living underground. Londoners are gregarious. They like to be in a crowd.

I'll have to admit that the people I've seen in many shelters seemed to be making a picnic of it. Also, people have a feeling that the more of them there are together, the safer they are.

I was in a good-sized room that was only half-filled, and the people were grumbly and unhappy. The marshal said that if you'd pack fifty people in there they'd be as happy as June bugs.

Some people, of course, do prefer the quiet and privacy of the smaller public shelters, where just a few people can sit around, sew, play cards and talk.

I went into one basement that held only two dozen people, and they had a piano. They were all singing when I walked in. And they happened to be singing "Marching Through Georgia."

In Soho I visited two or three shelters in the basements of small office buildings. They were cozy and pleasant, and you had at least a feeling of privacy. In the small shelters you can fix up a bunk in a corner with some permanency, and get a few little homey things around you.

People often go long distances to sleep in their favorite shelters. They say people travel by bus and subway four or five miles to sleep in the big, jolly Double-X shelter; yet other people who live within two blocks of Double-X will travel four or five miles nightly by tube to sleep underground at Marble Arch.

Although people in all the public shelters have to take their bedding home every morning, "guests" in some shelters are so permanent that they are allowed to install their own iron beds and chairs. You see whole rows of deep old leather chairs right out of the sitting rooms at home, with old people sitting up asleep in them. And there are hundreds of canvas deck chairs that people sleep in all night.

Whenever, late in the afternoon, you see somebody with a cheap brown suitcase going down the street, he is on his way to a shelter for the night. I wish I had been in the cheap-brown-suitcase business this past year. You even see people going to shelters in taxis, but with their cheap brown suitcases.

At Double-X you see hundreds of baby buggies parked around the walls. They didn't bring babies; they brought bedding. Officials think they may be forced to forbid baby buggies, for people bring so much stuff in them. It takes up too much room. Some people come practically ready to set up housekeeping.

I was amazed at the number of soldiers in the shelters. That seemed dreadful to me. A soldier comes home on a few days' leave for some life, liberty and a little fling at happiness. And then, because his home has gone or his folks have moved, he has to spend his leave lying on a dungeon floor.

However, not all the soldiers go to shelters because they have to. Lots of them go there to pick up girls. And officials at Double-X hint that some of the girls are not of the whitest virtue. The wardens worry about this; but virtue or not, I will say that there are girls at Double-X in the poor East End who are the loveliest I have seen in all London.

Incidentally, the girls over here are wearing coats with those Alaska-type parkas, of the same material, that pull over the head. And they look snappy.

Many people, after trying the new shelter bunks installed by the government, go back to the floor. The bunks are less than two feet wide, and too short for comfort. On the floor, people have room to stretch and roll around.

Most of the bunks are three-deckers. Those in the tube stations are made of steel. All the rest are of wood, pegged together at the joints so they can easily be knocked down and moved. They are unfinished, and look very home-made. Some have slat bottoms, others canvas bottoms.

The other night I was in a shelter that had not had the bunks installed yet, and the marshal said the people had taken a vote and only two out of the three hundred wanted bunks. But they have to take them anyway, for the Ministry of Health says so.

A few people, in the better shelters, bring pajamas and put them on before going to bed. But they are very few. Most people sleep with all their clothes on, even their hats. I have been surprised at how few slacks I've seen on women. I should think they would be ideal for shelter sleeping.

Before leaving home I was told by a British friend to bring a ski suit. He said it was just the thing for jumping into quickly, and for shelter wear. But I've been practically living in shelters for a week, and I haven't seen a ski suit yet. Anyway, I would feel sort of silly stretched out here on a deep sofa in room 672 of the Savoy Hotel in a ski suit.

3. STARS AND STRIPES

London,
February, 1941.

A lot of mighty fine sacrificing is being done in the bomb shelters of London.

I don't care where you go, whether to one of the vast corral-like shelters or to a small neat one in the West End, there is somebody there who is giving his time and his strength and his heart for his fellow humans.

Take one big basement shelter in the East End which holds around three thousand people. There in that vast hotel of sorts is a tiny, dwarfed man named Mickey Davis. He comes only to my waist. You have to lean over when you talk to him.

He has not been out of that shelter since last September except for an occasional walk. He works day and night. And he doesn't get a cent for it. People idolize him.

"There's something queer about living underground," he told me. "You stay down here so long you don't even want to go outside. Then when you do go out and get accustomed to the fresh air again you don't want to come back down."

There are thousands and thousands of "Davises" serving these harassed people of London.

I have a friend who works as an accountant all day and then serves most of the night as a shelter marshal, without pay. I've seen girls who clerk all day in a ten-cent store and then go to an East End shelter to serve thousands of people over the canteen counter till ten o'clock at night. And they are up at five in the morning to serve early tea and coffee. They do that every night, and they get no pay for it. In the West End I saw women of comfortable means who go every night to sit on stools and make sandwiches by the thousands to be sold to the shelterers at cost.

Britain's civil army has its big blitz heroes who are the greatest this war has produced. But it also has its little heroes by the tens of thousands. I think it's lots harder to be a little hero, because you have to keep so everlastingly at it.

Back in September, shelter management was in a state of chaos. They were just learning then. So great were the crowds that women would fold up their bedding and go out the front door of a shelter at eight o'clock in the morning, and then turn right around and stand there all day in line, waiting to get back through the same door at four that afternoon.

But now the population of each shelter is pretty well settled down into permanent residence. Also, each section or bay of a shelter is somewhat self-governing. A deputy marshal, chosen by the people, knows everybody in his particular bay, and where they sleep, so they no longer have to wait in line. The marshal reserves space for them.

All these deputy marshals are volunteers, serving without pay. Chief marshals get about $13 a week, and how they work for it!

It was amazing and touching the way the Christmas spirit was kept up during the holidays. People banded together and got up Christmas trees, and chipped in to buy gifts all around. I visited more than thirty shelters during the holidays, and there was not a one that was not elaborately decorated.

In all the shelters used by Greeks, the people have fixed up composite pictures of King George of England and King George of Greece alongside each other. Every shelter has a flag and at least one big picture of the King and the usual "God Save Our Home" mottoes. And that brings me back to a little incident up at the vast and conglomerate Double-X shelter, which has a heavily Jewish population.

The shelter marshal there asked me if I knew where he could get an American flag.

"It's funny your coming here tonight," he said, "for I just had that request this morning. Most of the people here have relatives in the States. They want an American flag. They say England and America are the only two countries left in the world."

Well, I'm not much on flags, but I figured it was up to me. So I went down to Selfridge's, bought the last American flag they had and took it out to Double-X.

The next day the shelter marshal called up, practically agog with gratitude, and said the people had made a great fuss over it. He said the women had started already making copies of it to hang all over the place. He said he had put twenty-four Greeks from a torpedoed merchant ship in that bay the night before, and they cheered when they saw the flag.

So I guess Ernest has done his good deed for 1941. The flag cost $2.50 too. I'm all torn now over whether I should be a hero and pay for it myself, or be a heel and put it on my expense account. I guess maybe I'll wait until I can be a more expensive heel.

I want to tell you about two remarkable shelters in London. Both of them come under the head of private group shelters. They are not open to the public.

The first one I saw, I was taken into privately and half surreptitiously, for few people even know that it exists. It must be one of the safest shelters in all London. It is in the basement of an apartment building, in a business section, and there is a bank on the ground floor. The shelter is the basement vault of the bank.

They've spent more than $10,000 fixing it up. Not a cent of this went for fancy trimmings, for the shelter isn't fancy at all. Every penny went for the physical strengthening of this vault.

There are five stories of strong building above the vault, and the ceiling of the vault itself is five feet of concrete. The vault consists of two rooms. In the smaller one, concrete has been added to make the ceiling eight feet thick. The walls are more than three feet thick. The doors are of heavy steel. On two sides of the vault are hallways, and beyond these another thick wall. Surrounding all four walls is old Mother Earth.

An elaborate arrangement of huge cogwheels manipulates a heavy steel trapdoor in the ceiling. This is an emergency escape door. Above this door, which leads to the ground floor, is the heaviest table I ever saw. Its legs are oaken posts a foot thick, and it has a heavy steel top to keep debris from choking down on top of the door.

The steel doors of the vault close on rubber strips, which make it gas-proof. If the lights are knocked out there is an auxiliary lighting plant, run from batteries. The ordinary escape doors out in the hall have been shored up with lengths of railroad iron to support debris.

At the door of the Savoy Hotel's shelter a man in a tuxedo sits at a desk. He checks in those residents of the hotel who wish to sleep in the shelter.

Inside, the shelter is softly lighted and quiet as a grave. It is air-conditioned. Great heavy satin draperies hang at the doorways, and other draperies divide the shelter into bays holding about twenty beds each. There is a wide aisle down the center, and the curtains make it all resemble a gigantic Pullman car made up for the night.

The beds are soft and deep. They have mattresses of the same type as are found in the regular hotel rooms. The linen is fresh.

There is a separate lounge in one corner where you can sit in deep chairs at tables and drink coffee. Just one floor up is a small bar.

The whole shelter is shored up with an intricate framework of heavy steel piping to brace the ceiling against the weight of bomb debris. At the entrance are three separate doors, one after the other, and each has a gas-proof curtain that can be lowered.

The shelter has its own maids and porters. It also has a full Red Cross unit, manned by seven part-time nurses. During the early September raids they treated many bomb casualties brought in off the streets.

The Savoy shelter can sleep more than two hundred people. Many of the hotel's guests sleep there every night, whether there's a raid or not.

Single men and single women are assigned separate bays, and there are bays for married couples. And carrying shelter etiquette to the nth degree, they even have a separate compartment for chronic snorers. They just herd 'em all together and let 'em snore it out. In fact, when the blitz first started, and before they hit on the idea of segregating the noisy ones, the hotel had one man on its night staff whose sole duty was to go around and shake up snorers!

4. LOOKING AHEAD

London,
February, 1941.

As a whole, life in London's public air-raid shelters reminds me of nothing so much as our own makeshift depression camps at home.

They sprang up suddenly out of a desperate need and amid considerable chaos. Like our camps, they are gradually getting better. As in our Okie camps, the people have set up a form of self-government. They elect their own leaders, and they have committees and representatives who sit on higher councils for making shelter rules and demanding better conditions — and God knows there is plenty of room for better conditions in some of the shelters.

The body heat of thousands of packed people makes some shelters stifling. In others, deep beneath stone arches and with concrete floors, the chill dampness is deadly. At one church in Stepney, people were actually sleeping until recently in stone coffins that once held corpses.

It wasn't until my second week of visiting shelters, when I was taken purposely to certain places, that I saw what a modernized shelter can begin to look like.

Let us take the Borough of Stepney as an example of what they are trying to do. This borough of a quarter of a million people has 300 shelters. They are not at regular intervals, but they are never many blocks apart. Most of them are not marked. At night you have to know ahead of time which door to go in. It is possible to walk along a dark sidewalk at night right past a door behind which there are lights and three thousand people and not realize that there is a soul within miles.

All these basements are leased by the borough. When the blitz started they weren't ready, and ever since they've been working on these basements right in the midst of all the people, trying to make them more habitable. But now Stepney has a program. More basements are constantly being rented and converted into shelters. When the program is finished, if it ever is finished, they hope to have 500 shelters.

Both for safety from bombs and for reasons of health, they want to disperse — to get the shelters thinned out. Under the new program they pick a strong basement, then work on it for weeks until it is fully ready before letting anybody in. At first it is shored up with a maze of brick walls, which also divide the basement into rooms housing twenty or thirty people each. Then wooden bunks are installed in rows. The ceilings are sealed with concrete so water can't seep through. The floors are concreted, if they were not already. A first-aid room is installed, with medical supplies. Banks of modern private toilets are built. Some shelters will even have shower baths, for the disinclination of poor people to bathe is worrying the doctors. Canteens are installed so the shelterers can get something warm at a reasonable price. Last, and best of all, a system of forced ventilation is put in. It is really air-conditioning — it can blow in either hot or cold air, and suck out dead air.

That is what Stepney is aiming at. And other boroughs are doing the same. When all this program is finished, London's shelters will be quite habitable underground dormitories. But right now too many of them are little better than underground Hoovervilles.

The churches have really done a great work in this shelter emergency. Many thousands of people are spending their nights in the lower depths of strongly built churches. In fact, of all the public shelters I have seen I like best the one in the basement of the Church of St. Martin's-in-the-Fields, in Trafalgar Square.

This old church is known to all American tourists who have been in London. Until a year and a half ago its extensive crypts were filled with the bones of the ancient dead. But the rector had these taken out and buried elsewhere about eighteen months ago, preparatory to using these rooms for social activities. They got the job finished just in time for the war. The newly emptied crypts made perfect air-raid shelters. And that is what they are today.

The crypts are filled with double-decked bunks. Central heating has just been installed. Also banks of private toilets. Everything is clean. There is a separate crypt for mothers with small babies. There is an all-night restaurant for people in uniform. There is a canteen for civilians.

You don't have to listen to a mission sermon, either. There are billiard and pingpong tables in the big central hall. It is more like a clubhouse than a church.

St. Martin's can sleep 500 people. Although it is in the rich West End, anybody can come. And anybody does — well-dressed men of the world, old Jewish mothers, soldiers, girls, and a great run of just average people like you and me.

You warm to St. Martin's as you do to a new acquaintance whom you like immensely. There is character here.

When you see a church with a bomb hole in its side and 500 fairly safe and happy people in its basement, and girls smoking cigarettes inside the sacred walls without anybody yelling at them, then I say that church has found a real religion.

Before I started over here I had a horror of being caught in some big wartime epidemic this winter. Well, it hasn't happened. So far, England's wartime health apparently is excellent. How or why, I don't know; for it seems to me that with a fourth of London's population crammed into holes beneath the earth's surface an epidemic would be a setup.

It's true that the city has been full of colds this winter. Many people who use the air-raid shelters suffer from something called "shelter throat." There is always much coughing — heavy coughing. I've had my cold, along with the rest. It kept me in bed for nearly a week, and I didn't feel so good. But I wasn't half as sick that week as I was the day I got my doctor's bill — $38.

Scarlet fever and diphtheria have actually shown a decline this winter. Pneumonia is up just a little. There has been no outbreak of real influenza. Typhoid has caused no worries. The only disease that has really gone up is cerebrospinal meningitis, known as spotted fever. This has jumped from 1500 cases in 1939 to 12,500 cases in 1940.

Right now London is in the midst of its most critical two winter months, and the doctors are keeping their fingers crossed, knocking on wood and throwing salt in seven directions. If they can go another month they'll be over the winter hump, and if they do get through without an epidemic I think they should salaam three times to Allah — and then start on preparations for next winter.

Those shelters have got to be improved faster than they are being improved now, regardless of cost. An epidemic in London might give Hitler the opening he's waiting for. These people simply can't go on living through winters this way without grave trouble. It seems to me that before another winter every big shelter must have a system of forced ventilation, sanitary toilets, adequate heating and warmer floors. They must be made dry. They must have better medical departments.

They did the best they could this winter. The biggest shelters have nurses. There are some doctors on duty. But most of the smaller ones have nothing of this sort. I visited one where the people themselves had chipped in to buy a medical kit; and the shelter marshal, who knew nothing at all about medicine, was acting as doctor and nurse. In another, the medical box was padlocked, and whoever had the key hadn't been around for days.

I remember reading a report by British doctors early last fall, saying that the lice and flea population of London was increasing alarmingly. I've asked about this at several of the poorest shelters, and so far as I can tell this increase has been halted. The smell of disinfectants is strong in all the big shelters, for they are cleaned and sprayed every morning. But, to my mind, they still aren't clean enough.

The first-aid rooms in the larger shelters are really miniature hospitals, staffed by Red Cross nurses and doctors who volunteer their services nightly. At the Double-X shelter I looked over their records for the last two months. About a fourth of the cases they had treated were of people suffering from boils. This seemed odd, so I asked about it, and one of the nurses said it was the result of the poor people's diet. Blood, toil, tears, sweat —and boils.

Shelter life in London, even at its best, is no bargain. I had thought I might find it exciting, or even romantic in spots, but I didn't. It seems to me there is something degrading to the human spirit in lying all night, crowded among other people, on a basement floor, within arm's reach of open toilets, in bad air and under constant supervision even on nights when no raid is in progress. I fear eventually it will do the same thing to weaken characters that being in prison does.

There are millions of people in London who prefer to take their chances in their homes, or somewhere else above ground. And I believe I am one of them.

PART VII: EXPEDITION TO THE NORTH

1. FEAR, WITH LAUGHTER

York,
February, 1941.

Yesterday I received notice that if I didn't get a move on I was to be expelled in disgrace from the Guild of Perpetual Travelers. So after six weeks of gathering moss in London, I packed my old sugar sack, shouldered my tin hat and gas mask, and hopped a northbound train to see how the war was getting on in the hinterland.

I took a 4 P.M. train out of London on the 160-mile ride to York. I got to the station half an hour early, and a good thing too, for within a minute after the train backed into the station there was hardly a seat left.

Easily two-thirds of the people on trains these days are in uniform. There are very few women. Soldiers on leave travel with full kit, including rifle. And a soldier with his full kit resembles a packhorse starting on a ten-day camping trip. They carry all this stuff because they must be ready at any moment. If the invasion comes while they're at home, they simply report to the nearest army post and start shooting.

You might think that with a war on, half the hotels in England would have to close. But it's just the opposite. The hotels have waiting lists, and if you don't make reservations ahead you are liable to find yourself homeless.

That nearly happened to me in York when I arrived at eight o'clock in the evening. If it hadn't been for a beautiful switchboard girl who called every hotel and boarding house in town I would have had to sit in the lobby all night. I fed her chocolates while she phoned, so we both profited.

Finally she found a place, a funny little semi-hotel that turned out to be grand. The owner was also the bellboy, and he built me a coal fire in the grate, put a hot-water bottle in the bed, and then stood and talked for half an hour.

There are many good-sized cities in England that haven't been blitzed yet. York has had only a few raids, and only a small number of people have been killed by bombs in this city of 85,000.

As we stood in my room talking, I said to the owner: "What shall I do about ventilation tonight? I can't open the blackout curtain with this fire going in the grate."

He answered, "Oh, this terrible old building is full of drafts. You'll get plenty of air without opening a window." And he was right.

Until nearly midnight I sat before my fireplace reading the newspapers. I felt very strange, way up here in York. The city, covered with snow and very quiet, seemed terribly old, and nice in a Dickens-like way. Although it was February, you somehow expected to see Santa Claus coming down the chimney.

The papers had grave editorials warning about the coming invasion attempt. I read and thought, and read and thought, here alone in my ancient room in old York, and a funny thing happened. I had been in London so long I had acquired the London outlook, the London casualness, the London assurance that no matter what happens we can stand it. The Londoner's psychology is like that of the aviator — somebody will get killed tonight, but it'll always be somebody else, never me. But now, away from my eight million friends in London, this psychological cloak of safety fell away. Here in these strange surroundings, among people not yet hardened to bombs, here where the warning siren is an event, the whole horrible meaning of invasion shone clear before me like a picture. The frightful slaughter that even an unsuccessful invasion would bring grew stark and real to me for the first time. And I tell you I became absolutely petrified with fear for myself. I would have given everything I had to be back in America.

I probably wouldn't have slept a wink if it hadn't been for the bathroom. I discovered it after midnight, when everybody else had gone to bed.

The bathroom was about twenty feet square, and it had twin bathtubs! Yes, two big old-fashioned bathtubs sitting side by side with nothing between, just like twin beds.

Twin bathtubs had never occurred to me before. But having actually seen them, my astonishment grew into approval. I said to myself, "Why not?" Think what you could do with twin bathtubs. You could give a party. You could invite the Lord Mayor in for tea and a tub. You could have a national slogan, "Two tubs in every bathroom."

The potentialities of twin bathtubs assumed gigantic proportions in my disturbed mind, and I finally fell asleep on the idea, all my fears forgotten.

Some friends drove me over to Harrogate, which is one of England's flossiest spas. It is some twenty-five miles from York.

Harrogate has curative waters, outlandishly huge hotels with prices so high they are famous, and in war or peace a stream of wealth and titles that stuns you.

Into this display of ease a German raider came, in daytime, and the people all stood in the street watching, thinking it was a British plane. They changed their minds when a bomb came down.

I asked if Harrogate had underground public shelters like London's and a slightly cynical English newspaper friend of mine said: "Yes, but nobody ever goes into them. Harrogate is so flossy that everybody is afraid of being seen in a public shelter in the presence of someone who isn't his equal."

English place names fascinate me. There is a street in York called Whipma Whopma Gate Street.

I went down to the tiny lounge of my hotel and sat in front of the fire with six other guests for late tea.

This little hotel is the only place I've been in — outside of an officers' mess — where they've had sugar in a bowl on the table, instead of just a cube for your coffee. The owner said he had found that by just leaving it out like that, putting people on their honor, guests used only half the sugar they did in peacetime.

There were two traveling salesmen at the hotel — one who sold shoes, and one who sold bread. One of them was from Sheffield, which was badly blitzed just before Christmas, and he had his wife and two boys with him. Due to the blitz, the youngsters had a six-week vacation from school, so they weren't feeling so hard toward the fortunes of war.

These two boys were much more interested in asking about streamlined trains in America than in telling about Sheffield's blitz. They have never been on a train. But they have studied mechanical magazines, and they told me all about the famous Royal Scot and Silver Jubilee streamliners.

When we did talk about bombing, I found that they knew as much about the characteristics of the various bombs as any air warden I've talked with. Yet the recent Sheffield blitz didn't seem paramount in their minds at all.

Traveling salesmen have a tough time now. They can get plenty of orders but they can't get the goods to fill them, because most of the factories are engaged in war work. Also, their gasoline is rationed. They're allowed from five gallons a month upward, depending on how useful the government considers them. And they try not to do much night driving, for it is not so pleasant in the blackout. Yet, despite all this and despite the snowy roads and despite the fact that England is thickly populated and the speed limits are low, these traveling salesmen will do 200 miles in a day when they can get gas.

These two were on the road the next morning by daybreak.

Some friends and I, in a York pub, got into a conversation with a native Yorkshireman, and I couldn't understand a word he said. I wouldn't have let on, except that the friends with me were all British soldiers and they couldn't understand him either. So finally we got into one of those long ridiculous discussions, the way you do in pubs, with us trying to analyze his talk and him trying to analyze ours. We all had a wonderful time — probably much better than if we had understood each other.

Not all Yorkshiremen talk the way this one did; not even a majority. Only on farms and in two or three other instances have I had trouble understanding Yorkshiremen. After I got home that night, and was still thinking about that fellow, the awful thought occurred to me that maybe he wasn't speaking a local dialect at all, but simply couldn't talk plain.

2. YORKSHIRE FARM

Borough bridge, Yorkshire,
February, 1941

The farmers of Yorkshire are getting a big play in the newspapers right now. For England realizes that she has got to turn this island into a big farm, what with Hitler trying to starve her to death by blockade. So I have been looking around some of the farms up here in Yorkshire.

The English farmer has had a terrible time since the last war. His standard of living has been abominably low. They say it is an amazing thing that anybody stayed on the farm at all.

The government did help a little, though not as much as ours has done. But now the government is doing things about the farms. It supplies loans, controls some prices, and in certain places does practically everything for the farmer except sitting on the fence and chewing a straw. But even so, the farm situation seems to me to be still fairly chaotic.

The main point is to get as much new land planted as possible. In many places they are plowing up cricket fields and golf courses. Every city and village has its "allotment plots," where townspeople with other jobs use their spare time working small patches in the city park, raising vegetables.

Despite England's dense population, plenty of land is available. For example, the West Riding of Yorkshire in 1938 had roughly 750,000 acres in grass, and only 250,000 acres of tilled land. But in 1940 and 1941 more than 100,000 acres of this grassland has been plowed up and planted. Over here they call it "plowing out." The old days of the great landholding squire with scores of tenants have pretty well passed since the last war. A majority of farm land is now owned in plots of about forty acres.

There is a hue and cry against the government right now for including farm hands in the next call-up for the army. The critics contend that the farms need all the experienced men they have, and that the army doesn't need men at all. A "women's land army" has been formed for work on the farms. It has 9000 members now, and another thousand are being recruited.

I dropped in to see one Yorkshire farm family. They are not exactly typical, for they live on government land and are much better off than most English farmers.

The head of the house is Robert Wray, who is getting along in years. He wears leather boots, and a shirt with a collar button but no collar. He has rheumatism and stays in the house on snowy days such as this one was. His son Richard does the work, and will until he is called up for the army. Mr. Wray's daughter, who was down on her knees scrubbing the floor when I was there, had just been married and was still very blushy about it.

The Wrays have sixty acres, and practically a model house and barn, built by the government. They pay an annual rental of $4 an acre, and their yearly income is about $800.

They live three miles from town, and they don't have a car or electric lights or a telephone. They live mostly in the kitchen in winter, but their kitchen is nicer than most farm kitchens. Instead of a regular cookstove, they have an open coal grate with ovens built into the wall beside the grate.

They have a bathroom, with nothing in it but a bathtub. When I looked in, there was three inches of water in the tub, and it was partly frozen over. The toilet is an old-fashioned one in a fuel shed a few steps back of the house. Every room in the house, including the bedrooms, has a small coal grate, but these are seldom lighted.

The house in brick. Practically all English farmhouses are brick or stone, for timber is scarce. The barn is concrete, and the very last word. The Wrays keep about thirty head of cattle, a dozen pigs, a few chickens and no sheep. They farm with horses. All the stock is kept in separate stalls, spread deep with straw.

The war seems remote from the Wray farm, yet they are in it along with all the rest of England. Their home is never likely to be bombed, but they will feel a drastically tightening economy, and harder work, and one by one the absence of kith and kin who go away to fight.

On a wall of the Wray sitting room are two framed pictures. They are photographs of the young bride's two uncles, in World War uniforms. One of them never came back from the last war. And before this one is over there will be more pictures of fighters on the wall — husbands, brothers and cousins. For everybody is in it, one way or another.

3. VISIT TO SCOTLAND

Edinburgh,
February, 1941.

Traveling through the countryside of Great Britain these days is hardly an undiluted pleasure. The bad points of traveling include: crowded trains and delayed schedules, if you're going by rail; snowy roads, unmarked highways and a shortage of gasoline, if you're driving; packed hotels, few taxis, and, worst of all, hotels that are unheated despite the fact that the north of England is nearer to the Arctic Circle than Newfoundland is. On the other hand, there are good points: warm trains, good food, pleasant companions, beautiful snow-covered scenery, and the fact that people will always help if you ask them. Bad as the drawbacks sound, you do get where you're going, and with surprising speed and comfort.

There is actually more rail traffic now than in peacetime, but of course this increase is in freight trains. Passenger service has been cut down, but not as much as I had thought. There are thirty passenger trains daily from London to Scotland. The trains are terrifically long and they are always packed.

There are no restrictions on travel in England. You don't have to get special permission or anything of that sort. You just get on a train and go. I've never had to show my multitudinous special papers since the day I got them. When I register at a hotel I have to put down my nationality, my passport number, where I've just come from and where I'm going. The English do too, except that instead of a passport number they put down their national registration number.

The better trains carry restaurant cars at dinner time. The diners are nicer than ours at home, with deep easy chairs. They bring you soup, lamb, boiled potatoes, cabbage, canned fruit and coffee for about eighty-five cents. Eating is pleasant on an English train.

For a stranger like me, it is hard to know when you get to where you're going. You almost never see a conductor or a porter. Only occasionally do they call out a station, and the names have been taken off most of the stations in order not to give pointers to the Germans if the invasion comes. At night, of course, the train windows are blacked out so you can't see the station you're coming into, anyway.

I've worked out a scheme of eavesdropping until I spot somebody who is going where I'm going, and then when he starts putting on his coat to get off I start putting on mine.

Some people know the railroad by heart. The other night, on the way from London to York, our train slowed down and we all thought we were coming into York.

"Wait a minute," said a man in our compartment. "I'll tell you in a minute."

He sat listening as the train crept forward. Suddenly we could tell we were crossing a bridge.

"No, this is not York," the man said. "This is Selby."

From the time we left London, four hours earlier, he had never looked up from his book, but just from the sound of the wheels he knew exactly where we were. That's what living in the blackout does to your senses.

In some railroad stations there are porters to help with your bags, and in some there are not. It is tough on a stranger getting to his destination at night — and I seem to arrive everywhere at night. You get off the train and there you are — all alone in a strange city, not knowing in which direction to go, everything black, and no taxis available. You just have to stand around helplessly until you dig up somebody with a kind heart.

It was nearly midnight when we got into Edinburgh, and it was snowing and cold. The station was a mad-house of soldiers. I never saw so many in my life, outside of a camp. A lone taxi would arrive about every five minutes, and somebody else would get it. Finally, after about a half hour, I did get one.

Friends had told me about a hotel which they said was the warmest in Edinburgh. I'm glad they didn't direct me to the coldest one, for my room had no heat whatever. It was like a refrigerator car. So the maid came at midnight and built a fire in the grate, plugged in a little electric heater and put a hot-water bottle in my bed. The grate fire, incidentally, costs fifty cents a day extra, the electric heater thirty cents.

I asked the maid to awaken me at eight in the morning and build another fire when she arrived. So when she knocked, before daylight, I reached over to unlock the door, as it was close to my bed. But the door wasn't as close as I thought, and I kept reaching outward in the dark and finally reached too far, lost my balance and fell right out of bed onto the floor and sprained a thumb.

As I lay there in the dark on the cold floor, tangled up in bed covers, freezing to death, my thumb hurting, there all alone in a pitch-black icebox in Scotland with not a friend within four hundred miles, I thought: Of all the damn fools I've ever heard of, you take the prize. For you could be in Panama or Hawaii now if you had any sense.

But I haven't any sense, and in spite of everything, I'm glad I'm here.

Edinburgh is a graceful city. It is the Washington or the Ottawa of Scotland. It is a city of government. It is a planned city. And it is the sturdiest city I have ever seen. In its buildings, I mean. Everything is of massive stone, so massive and so heavy that the entire municipality seems embedded in the rock underfoot.

It seems to me that Edinburgh would stand up physically under an aerial blitz better than any other city in Britain. They haven't had one yet, and if they ever do, it will be the rankest of outrages, for Edinburgh is not an industrial city.

Many things are different up here. There is more food than in London, and a greater variety of it. You have no trouble getting an excellent steak.

Some people say Edinburgh is the gayest city in Britain now. There are beautiful restaurants, where Scottish officers dancing in kilts make a picture.

You never see a civilian with a tin hat or a gas mask. Edinburgh children were evacuated, but eighty per cent of them have come back. The movies run at night as well as in the daytime. Nobody sleeps at night in public shelters, although shelters are available.

I have friends here who travel to London weekly and who know what has happened down there. These friends get disgusted with their home folks when they return.

"Up here we are all complaining about our stomach aches and rheumatism," they say. "It sounds mighty trivial when you have just come from London, where they really have got something to complain about — and don't. I think a little blitzing would do us good."

True, Scotland has not been on the receiving end of many bombs. True also, there is a certain fundamental dislike of England, but that goes by the boards in an emergency. Their heart is in the war all right. I have got the impression that if I were an invading German, or even a fire bomb, I wouldn't relish the job of trying to land on Scottish soil.

As far as I can see, Edinburgh's past immunity to danger has not made it lax. The city seems to be ready and waiting. It is organized in every way. Its officials have visited blitzed cities to study what has happened and have prepared accordingly.

For example, much of Edinburgh lives in small apartment houses that they call tenements. Because of this municipal singularity, the Air Raid Precaution service is different from that in other cities. Edinburgh is organized tenement by tenement — a warden for each tenement, and he is on duty right there all the time.

I like the Scottish people. Somehow I had them all wrong. For one thing, I thought I wouldn't be able to understand anything they said, but they are easy to understand. Also, I thought they were dour. On the contrary, they are fundamentally witty. It is hard for a Scotsman to go five minutes without giving something a funny twist, and it is usually a left-handed twist. All in all, I have found the Scots much more like Americans than the Englishmen are. I feel perfectly at home with them.

And incidentally, just a couple of tips in case you ever come over here: (1) Don't refer to Scotland as if it were a part of England, as I did; for it isn't. England is England, and Scotland is Scotland. (2) Don't say Scotch unless you are referring to the whisky. People are Scots, and they are Scottish but not Scotch.

Incidentally, Scotch whisky is getting short. Many bars limit their customers to two drinks. The whisky is being sent to America for good American dollars to spend on arms.

It seems that one Scotsman was telling another about being in a movie theater when some German raiders came over. The manager stopped the film, went onto the stage and announced, "The sireens has went."

It was now time for the other Scotsman to laugh, but he didn't. He studied it over for a long time, then finally laughed and said, "I suppose the joke of it was that the sireens hadna' went?"

4. A SCOTTISH FAMILY

Newhaven, Scotland,
February, 1941.

As far back as he can remember, Walter Rutherford's folks have been fishermen. But his father said he would rather see his sons dead than see them become fishermen, so they became such things as engineers and shopkeepers.

But Walter stayed close to the sea. Newhaven is a fishing village, and Walter runs the shop that outfits the fishermen. He is a ship chandler.

For twelve years he has been president of the Fishermen's Society, a proud organization that goes back to 1648. Packed in a shoebox at his house are the beautiful silver cups and medals that go with the honor. Mrs. Rutherford has sung in the Fisherwomen's Choir since she was a girl. This choir is famous, and often travels to London to sing.

I was a guest at the Rutherfords for an evening — at my own invitation, but nobody could have been treated more genuinely if he had been kith and kin. I went to see them in order to find out whether the war was really close to the average family in Scotland. And people assured me the Rutherfords were typical.

Well, when the war came Walter turned over his ship chandler's shop to Mrs. Rutherford and went to work in a factory that makes marine engines for the government. He is a gauge maker — the same trade he followed at Glasgow in the last war. He had been out of it eighteen years, but he is at it again now.

Walter is a grandfather, yet he gets up at 6 a.m. and rides a bicycle to work in the dark — for during the winter it isn't daylight here until nine o'clock in the morning. That is, he did ride a bicycle, but he is walking now. The other morning his front wheel hit a curb and he took a spill, landing in the snow "right on my bottomside," as he says.

Walter works twelve hours a day, with only one day off every two weeks.

"Those are mighty tough hours," I said.

"They are tough for a man who is getting along," he said.

Mrs. Rutherford laughs about his "getting along." For he looks about thirty-five. He has a ruddy, windy face without a single line in it. He wears a turtle-neck sweater and hops around like a jumpingjack.

"I'm always being taken for his mother," Mrs. Rutherford laughs. "But I don't mind."

Mrs. Rutherford is a large woman, and she is straight up and down no matter whether she is standing or sitting. She has enough humor for a dozen Scotswomen. She keeps long hours in the chandler's shop, which is under their apartment on the street floor.

"Sometimes I just feel like closing it up," she says, "and other times I'm thankful I have it to keep me from thinking."

And believe me, she has plenty to think about. Her boy, who is her pet, was a fish auctioneer, but now he is in the R.A.F. in Malta. Her son-in-law was a fisherman but is now in a naval patrol, feeling his way around among the mines. Her other daughter's fiance is a dispatch rider with the Fusiliers. They were just ready to get married, but it's off now till after the war.

And the children's best friend, just down the street, also went from fishing into the naval patrol. A few weeks ago his boat hit a mine. They could hear the explosion from the chandler's shop. His young wife was in the shop and heard it too. They never found anything of him at all.

"It was seven weeks after our boy left for Malta before we heard from him," Mrs. Rutherford says. "I would come up here from the shop and cry by the hour with a broken heart, but finally we got a cable from him."

Everybody in this village has somebody in the war.

Mrs. Rutherford is so impetuous she can't stay sad very long, and so honest she says just what she thinks. She has no, inhibitions. She is a good deal like my own mother. Walter tells how one night recently she was listening to someone speaking on the radio from America, talking about liberty and how we must give all aid to Britain, and suddenly Mrs. Rutherford yelled at the radio, "Oh shut up! Stop talking so much and do something!"

The Rutherfords are neither poor nor very well off. The chandler's shop has put their three children through school and has bought them a house and car. The car is laid up now, for Walter works all day and Mrs. Rutherford doesn't drive.

"But you are not going to sell that car," says Mrs. Rutherford. "It's going to be right here for the boy when he gets back. It's a bonnie wee car."

The Rutherfords both use "wee" and "bonnie" almost constantly. Such native expressions sound odd alongside their modern slang phrases, such as "fed up."

For "herring," Mrs. Rutherford says what sounds like "hen." Being in a fishing village, they have to eat an awful lot of fish. "It's just hen, hen, hen, morning, noon and night," she says.

The Rutherfords never miss church, but they are far from being churchy people.

Their home is in what we would call a cooperative apartment. They own the first and second floors of one section of a brick building. They have two bedrooms, a kitchen and bath. As in many Scottish houses, the kitchen also serves as a living room. There is a parrot in a cage by a blacked-out window.

At ten-thirty the youngest girl, who lives at home, came in from a movie. Then Mrs. Rutherford put on the coffeepot, got out a jar of cakes and made sandwiches. We all sat around the kitchen table and ate and talked. I never felt more at home in my life.

5. THE RED CLYDE

Glasgow,
February, 1941.

Edinburgh is on the east side of Scotland and Glasgow on the west, but since they are at Scotland's narrowest point they are only an hour's ride apart by train. The country between looks very much like Indiana, except that the fields are smaller here.

That's the trouble with America — it's so big and has so many kinds of scenery that it makes all the other countries look like something at home, instead of looking foreign.

Edinburgh is cultured, scholarly, historical and quiet. Glasgow is industrial, cosmopolitan, pulsating and full of business. They are as different as two cities could be.

Sailors have told me that they found Glasgow the warmest city on the Seven Seas, as far as making you welcome was concerned. Personally, I could see no difference along that line between the two cities. I was chilled physically and warmed spiritually by both of them.

We got off the train at Glasgow, checked our bags and took a walk. In sight of the station was a building wrecked by a bomb — one of the very few in Glasgow. The only casualties were two people who started to walk downstairs in the dark after the blast; the stairs weren't there.

Glasgow has not had a blitz. They have expected one all along, for they have factories and great shipyards. The people can't understand why Hitler hasn't tried to give it the works. Some say he is saving the shipyards for himself — after he seizes Ireland and swings across the Irish Sea. Others say very knowingly that he is saving them for something else, but they are so knowing that I never know what they mean.

We walked through a big park by the station, full of brick air-raid shelters exactly like the surface shelters in London. I went up to see what one was like inside, but its slatted door was solidly locked. My Scottish friend said, "That's just in case there is a raid and somebody wants to get inside."

We were already overdue at an appointment, but my friend said I would have to see how the businessmen of Glasgow work. So we went to a basement coffee house which was nearly a block long, with deep rugs and walls solid with framed paintings. The whole place was packed, with men sitting two and three at a table, their hats on, drinking coffee and talking. It was eleven o'clock in the morning.

My friend made up an imaginary conversation at a nearby table. "Now this is a sure-fire thing if I can just get hold of a little capital," one fellow was theoretically saying — and my friend said the chances were 10 to 1 he was actually saying just that. That's how business is done in Glasgow. It reminded me of Rio de Janeiro, where people go to work at ten and knock off at ten-thirty for a couple of hours of sidewalk coffee drinking.

Glasgow is prosperous now. It needs to be. It had a tough time through the depression — a black, dismal, dangerously tough time.

Glasgow is on the River Clyde, and all over Britain you hear of the "Red Clyde." They don't mean red with blood, they mean red with Communism. Glasgow is supposed to be the center of Communism in Britain. The Daily Worker had a Glasgow edition until it was suspended recently by the government.

I'm not a muckraker nor a political investigator, so my delvings into the Clyde's redness have not been deep. But I have got the same story from the rich and the poor and the middle-income man alike, and that is that the Clyde is not so red after all. Not even a small fraction of one per cent of the workers are Communists. They are just tough guys who are agin things as a matter of habit. They are agin their bosses, they are agin their political leaders, and they would be agin Stalin or agin Hitler if one of those gentlemen happened to be their boss. But there is no question with the men of Glasgow about who is going to win this war — that's Great Britain.

These fellows up here in the shipyards, the dockworkers down in Liverpool, the coal miners in Wales, the Cockneys in their London slums, and farmers all over Britain — they are the guys who will have to have a new deal when the war is over. They are the guys the country must make some war aims for when the victory is won.

The men of Glasgow drink big and talk hard. You see a shipyard worker go up to a bar in a Clydebank pub and he will say, "A glass and a half." You know what that means? It means a glass of beer and half a glass of whisky, the equivalent of two big slugs. He drinks the whisky, washes it down with the beer, and goes back to work.

We got aboard a Glasgow police launch for a private sightseeing excursion down the River Clyde, past the great shipyards.

The day was miserable and dark, with lowering clouds, cold and windy. Mist and smoke combined to make the same stuff they call "smog" in Knoxville. You can't keep a shirt clean in Glasgow either.

There are bridges across the Clyde in Glasgow, but none out toward the sea. However, there are frequent little ferries, in which the passengers stand up. These ferries are free, run by the city. "That," said the policeman at the wheel, "is for Aberdonians [people from Aberdeen]. They come down here on a holiday and ride back and forth all day."

All the world makes a byword of the Scotsman's thriftiness, but in Scotland itself they blame it all on people from Aberdeen.

And while we're on the point, I notice in Glasgow that your Scottish friends insist on paying for the first ones, and they always say, "No sir, you can't pay for anything in Scotland."

The River Clyde is not very wide, but on its two banks for several miles downriver is probably the greatest concentration of shipbuilding in the world.

One great shipbuilding yard after another — you can't begin to count the number of ships under construction. They run all the way from the mere ribworks of ships being started, which resemble dinosaur skeletons, on up to ships ready to be launched in a few days. And at the docks there is ship after ship, already launched but without superstructure yet, going through the process of being fitted for sea.

Several things impressed me about these shipyards. One was that ships look smaller in stocks than in the water. Another was that the stocks, instead of being at right angles to the river bank, were all built slantwise. That is because the river is so narrow the ships would scoot clear across the river on being launched and ram the other bank. So they set the stocks slantwise and launch the ships to slide upriver.

Stocks from which a ship was launched yesterday will have the keel of a new one started today.

From the river, the stocks where the Queen Mary and Queen Elizabeth were built don't look big enough to take a tramp steamer.

The stocks of a shipyard, instead of being a great permanent thing like a drydock, look scant and temporary, more like a high corral fence, except that huge movable cranes tower over each of them. Seen at a distance, this vast mass of cranes gives you the same feeling of density that the oil-well derricks do around Long Beach, California.

We were on the river for two hours. As we chugged back to our little dock I thought to myself: Yes, Britannia still rules the seas. And I also thought: But what about after the war — when all of these giant stocks stand empty, and instead of the miles-long rattle of riveting hammers there is a dead silence, and the thousands of men haunt the pubs for lack of anything else to do? What about the "Red Clyde" then?

After the river tour I had nothing to do for a couple of hours, so I took the opportunity to see "The Great Dictator," which is now showing all over Britain. It was three o'clock in the afternoon. The theater was a big one, but it was packed. It made you feel that the war wasn't real.

I wasn't very enthusiastic about the picture, and when Chaplin made his much discussed speech at the end it somehow made me embarrassed. People know all that over here already; that's what they've been fighting about for a year and a half; it seemed superfluous.

But the people of Glasgow cheered it heartily.

At Clydebank I made some new friends and spent an evening with them. They are good, normal, intelligent, Scottish working people. Their name is Roberts. They live in a brick-row house in a wide suburban street. They are a family of seven — a grandfather, his three grown children, a son-in-law and two little grandbabies.

William Roberts, the head of the house, was a needle straightener in a sewing-machine factory, but he is retired now. I never knew before that there was such a thing as a needle straightener.

Greta, the youngest daughter, now works in that same factory, but it doesn't make sewing machines any more — it makes munitions.

Willie, the son, used to work in the shipyards, but has tried to better himself through much study, reading and thinking. He works for the government now, making talks about war aims all over the country. The family laughs and calls him "The Professor." He farms a small allotment in a park a few blocks away.

The son-in-law is a plater in the shipyards.

Like good average people anywhere, the Robertses say what they think, and it isn't all in praise of the government. They are right in the midst of the details of war work, and details that are wrong loom large to them. They see inefficiency and waste and floundering organization, and they come right out with it. They sound just like people at home.

Greta said to me: "Do you suppose America will come in at the last minute again, and say she won the war?" Yet in spite of that crack we got along famously.

Greta once worked in London for three months; her greatest desire is to see Hawaii.

Her brother and I were a little late getting home, and we missed supper. So Greta threw together a snack of fried eggs and sausage. The rest of the family sat in front of the fireplace while we ate.

There was a jar of jelly on the table. I took some onto my plate and began putting it on some bread.

"Wait," Greta called, "that's jelly."

"Sure, I know it is," I said.

"But you're putting it on your bread!" she exclaimed.

"Of course," I said. "What should I do with it?"

"Why we eat it for dessert," she said. "I never heard of putting jelly on bread with your meal."

She laughed every time I took a bite.

No American had ever been in the Roberts' home before, and I think I amused them a great deal. They said I talked with a drawl just like the cowboys in the movies. Greta said she really expected me to go "Yippee!" every once in a while.

The Roberts family has an Anderson shelter back of the house. They have fixed it up with electric lights and a heater, but they have never had to use it. They appreciate the fact that they've been lucky, and they don't count on the luck lasting. They are ready for a raid when it comes, and they expect one.

At the fireside we got to discussing Mr. Churchill. Back in America I suppose we hear Churchill's name mentioned a dozen times a day, but when we started talking about him here it suddenly occurred to me that I had heard his name mentioned very seldom in England. I don't know why that is, for Britain idolizes him and certainly is behind him to a man. Yet they don't talk much about him, and I never yet have heard him referred to as "Winnie."

I thought the Roberts' feeling about Churchill was very revealing. All their critical talk about production and speed and British methods of warfare and so forth was just good democracy expressing itself. But their talk about Churchill showed where their real feelings lay.

The son-in-law, sitting on a couch, shook his head and said: "I don't know what would happen to us if we lost Churchill."

And the father, in a deep chair by the fire, said: "Yes, it would be bad. He's the man who pulled us together."

By then it was midnight and the last bus was about due, so I said good-bye and felt my way out into the Scottish night.

6. DEFENSE IN DEPTH

Paisley, Scotland,
February, 1941.

This is the city that used to make Paisley shawls. It wasn't until I came here that I discovered genuine Paisley shawls haven't been made in sixty years. That is, real hand-woven ones.

But America still knows this city, at least indirectly; for as one person expressed it, "Nearly all the buttons that hold up the pants of America are sewed on with thread from Paisley."

This is a great textile city, but it is neither shawls nor thread that I'm going to write about. It is the Home Guard.

You have heard about Britain's Home Guard, the civilian army which has sprung to arms to make an invasion of Britain impossible. There are today something like 1,700,000 men in the Home Guard, which came into existence in May, 1940. At first their organization was flabby and almost without direction. Today they are well equipped and well trained and, I can assure you, very formidable men.

They are here literally to defend their homes. Every city, town and village has its Home Guard. They drill, and practice marksmanship, and study plans. They are ready for whatever comes.

Today the whole force is uniformed. The uniform is brown, just like the regular army's, but they wear white armbands with the words "Home Guard." This may be abandoned, however, for in case of invasion the Germans could spot them too easily.

A large percentage of the Home Guard are World War veterans. Practically all the members have daytime jobs.

As we sat around a Home Guard post at night, drinking late tea, I asked the men around me what work they were in. There were three salesmen, an architect, a billposter and his assistant, a school janitor, a preacher, a truck driver, a schoolteacher and a lawyer.

The Paisley Home Guard has a strength of several thousand men. Every so often each man is on duty all night. He spends most of his duty night in cleaning guns, studying military tactics, and maybe drilling. There are a few cots, and the ones who have to go to work early in the morning are allowed to snatch a few winks. But for two hours every night each man is actually out in the dark patrolling — looking for parachutists or anything suspicious.

This patrol is maintained all over Britain by the Home Guard, every night, all night. They patrol in strength, so that if they should spot a German landing party one man could run back and give the alarm while the others held off the attackers until help came.

The Home Guard is essentially a deep-line defense. The way Britain figures it, the Navy and the Air Force are the first lines of defense against invasion. If Germany should break through these, behind them on the land is Britain's now formidable regular army and an intricate maze of defenses that would astound you. The fourth line of defense is the Home Guard, whose duty is to prevent infiltration by the enemy back of the front lines — the thing that has destroyed so many other countries.

They estimate that a planeload of parachutists, with everything planned perfectly, could jump out over Britain at night, collect into a group after landing and be ready with bicycles and machine guns to go into action within fifteen minutes. It is the Home Guard's job to see that they are spotted and wiped out before the fifteen minutes are up, or, failing in that, to hold them up until the regular army arrives on the scene.

They say there is no spot in Britain, no matter how isolated, that cannot be reached in force by the regular army within an hour.

Every street and every country road in all Britain is patrolled throughout the night by the Home Guard.

I have a friend who was driving along an east-coast road one night. It was isolated, bleak and lonesome country. He stopped for a moment on personal business, and stood looking toward the sea. Then he drove on a few miles, and stopped at a pub for a drink. While he was in the pub a Home Guardsman came up and required him to identify himself. Somebody had seen him out there in the darkness.

"And suppose," my friend asked, "suppose I hadn't stopped at this pub for a drink. What would you have done?"

"You wouldn't have got four miles," the guardsman replied. "You're being watched for right now at every crossroad in every direction from here."

The Home Guard which was not even in existence less than a year ago, today is well equipped.

Most of the Guard's arms have come from America. In one post I saw American rifles and machine guns. The Guard is well supplied with hand grenades. And the countryside is a network of tank traps and obstructions that even the local people don't see or recognize.

Provincial England is determined that the Germans shall not pass. Of course there is some good democratic bellyaching against the government, and derision about mistakes. There are thousands of hot-stove-league fighters who know how to run the war better. There are some shirkers, and no doubt even a few fifth columnists. And yet I suppose there never has been a nation more unanimous in its mind than Britain is now. If she ever stumbles in this war, I feel absolutely certain that it will not be by the immoral Quisling route.

Among the soldiers of Britain, and even among the bombed people of London, I have found very few who hate the Germans with the frenzy of World War days. But these middle-aged Home Guardsmen do. Most of them carry over their hate from the last war, and it is intensified by resentment at having to do the job all over again. It is further intensified by the fact that now they're fighting for their own homes and families, right in their own streets and their own fields and pastures.

In Home Guard posts you hear the terms "Boche" and "Hun" more often than you hear "Jerry." The Home Guardsmen say they intend to take no prisoners. They say they intend to use their bayonets when they get that close.

I don't know whether it has been definitely settled which is the stronger — steel or a man's spirit. I only know that Britain's Home Guard is armed with a state of mind that is likely to make parachuting a very unpleasant calling.

No doubt you've read that when the invasion comes the church bells will ring all over Britain. We were talking about this the other night at a Home Guard post, and as we talked I realized I had not heard a church bell since I came to England. It is, in fact, against the law to ring a church bell today in Britain. They've even stopped firing the famous one o'clock gun from the castle in Edinburgh, a custom there longer than anyone can remember.

Recently in one district of Paisley they had a surprise mobilization of the Home Guard at 6 a.m., which was long before daylight. Nobody but the leaders knew about it ahead of time.

They didn't ring bells. They just passed the word along from house to house. And with no prearrangement or warning at all, fifty men out of the membership of fifty-three in this section were at their stations inside of fifteen minutes.

I talked to a Home Guardsman who is sixty years old and has seven service medals. He has fought in Egypt, India and Africa. He was in the Boer War and the first World War. Now he is a billposter by day and a guardsman by night. On the side he is an informer for the Ministry of Information. And he has a son who went through Dunkirk. He just hopes the Germans will come — that's all he hopes.

I sat until 3 a.m. in front of a glowing fireplace with David McQueen, a Presbyterian minister here in Paisley.

The Church of Scotland, you know, is Presbyterian; and it used to be a part of the State. Presbyterian ministers here are highly educated in the classics. When you sit with Mr. McQueen you are sitting with a man of intellect.

Mr. McQueen is in the war. He has raised thousands of pounds for soldiers' entertainment. His church runs a canteen for the troops stationed here. Wounded R.A.F. fliers come to live with him in his manse, to recuperate. And Mr. McQueen is a private in the Home Guard.

They wanted to make him a padre for the Guard but he wouldn't do it. He said that if they did that then they should make the pipe organist a bandsman, and no band is needed. So on every duty night David McQueen, Presbyterian minister, is out in the dark fields in uniform, patrolling up and down, looking for Germans.

When his turn falls on Saturday night, he has to go right to church Sunday morning without a wink of sleep, and preach two sermons. He says he has to keep the church cold in order not to fall asleep while he's talking.

That's the Home Guard for you.

PART VIII: MURDER IN THE MIDLANDS

1. TRAIN TALK

On a Train in England,
February, 1941.

You can go from Scotland back to London, some 400 miles, on an overnight sleeper. Or you can take a sleeper to the industrial Midlands, which is where I'm going.

English sleepers are much pleasanter than most of ours. Every berth is in a separate compartment. It has a washbowl, plenty of mirrors, baggage racks, shelves, and room enough for a circus giant to undress. The compartment is air-conditioned, and you can keep warm and have fresh air all night without opening a window. If two people are traveling together they get two compartments with a connecting door. When the conductor awakens you in the morning he does so with a tray of hot tea and a package of cakes.

They say that before the war it was unheard of for one Englishman to speak to another on a train. But the war has broken that down. I have now made five trips by train, and only on one of them was I in a compartment where people didn't talk.

It is now quite good manners for men in uniform to start talking to each other. A question about some detail of traveling usually opens the conversation.

And as for me, after I've said a few words one of my fellow passengers is always sure to ask if I'm from Canada. I say no, America, and then we are off. They are all interested to know what the American public is feeling about the war. But I tell them I don't know, since sentiment apparently has changed since I left the States.

You'd be surprised how much they know about us in Scotland. I was actually ashamed, for I met hardly a Scotsman who didn't know twice as much American history as I do.

This new familiarity on the train is still a little hard for some aristocrats. The higher they go in the scale, the less talking they do.

The other evening I was in the dining compartment of a train, along with two naval officers, an army colonel and a Polish officer — all obviously gentlemen. And from the time I went in until I was having coffee more than an hour later, not a word was spoken by any of us six men sitting there beside each other.

Finally, toward the end, one of the naval officers offered the other a cigarette, and then offered one to me. We took a few puffs, and I said it was a good cigarette. The other naval officer said he liked it too. That was the sum total of that evening's conversation.

But between York and Newcastle I was in a compartment with a middle-aged civilian, an officer of the merchant marine and a very young commissioned officer of the Fusiliers, and we talked our heads off.

The civilian said he had traveled this thirty-mile stretch of railroad every day for twenty years. He lived in one town and worked at a factory in another. The night before he had been roof-spotting at his factory.

The merchant-marine officer was serving in convoys around the British Isles. He had been in Baltimore, Florida and Los Angeles, and said he'd like to live in America five or six years, but not permanently.

The young army officer was more than six feet tall, but looked as if he should have been in high school. Yet he was a veteran of Dunkirk, and he told us about those hectic days. He said he went two days and nights without sleep or food, but didn't miss either of them.

We were riding through a blizzard, and the train was nine hours late. These two men had been on the train eighteen hours without anything to eat, and they were about starved. The young fellow said he never got half as hungry at Dunkirk as he was now.

Both of these young men had been through stuff on land and sea where their lives for the moment were not worth a dime. Yet the thing that seemed to impress them most about the war was the way London takes the bombing. They had both been there on leave, and they said they could hardly believe the way London stands up to it.

Also we got to talking about conscientious objectors. They're called "conchies" over here. These two young fellows in uniform were completely tolerant of the conchies. They felt that if a fellow was sincere he should be allowed to do some kind of nonmilitary work.

The young officer ran out of cigarettes and kept smoking ours and apologizing. When the civilian got to his station he said good-bye and got off, but in a moment he was back pounding at the window. We opened it, and he handed the young officer a package of cigarettes.

The English are really proud of each other. Half a dozen times when I've been talking to strangers they've got off on the general subject of how Britain pulled herself together. And half a dozen times I've heard this same expression:

"They said we were decadent, and soft from easy living and the desire for peace. But I guess we're not decadent yet."

2. FACTORIES-EVERYWHERE

Birmingham,
February, 1941.

This is a city of more than a million people — the second largest city in England.

Since it is a manufacturing city, the Germans have tried to give it the works. They have made scars, but they haven't been able to obliterate Birmingham. The city is damaged in about the same proportion as London's West End, which is bad, but not bad enough for Hitler's purposes. Up to the moment, Birmingham is not a city that will have to be rebuilt after the war. It is a city that will just have to be patched up.

Birmingham has big factories, but it is also noted for its little ones. It is a city wherein the small individual plant still lives — where craftsmanship is a virtue. There are more than 2000 factories in Birmingham. That's why Hitler would almost have to wipe out the city before he could put Birmingham's production out of business.

Practically all of these factories are making something for the war. I went to visit one small plant. It was in a darkish old brick building, covering about an eighth of a block. Hitler could never find it unless he sent a man on a bicycle to ask a policeman.

Tom Waterhouse is owner and manager of this plant. It is what we at home would call a machine shop. And it is small industry at its best. There are only twenty-five employees, and their average service in this same concern is twenty-five years. As I went through the shop I asked the first four men I came to how long they had been with the company, and the answers were thirty-five, thirty-seven, forty and forty-five years.

"What do you make here?" I asked Mr. Waterhouse.

He laughed and said, "We make whatever nobody else wants to make. We make hundreds of crazy things — special parts for guns and marine engines and so on. There is no mass production here. Every piece is a special piece for a special purpose, and they're made practically by hand."

Mr. Waterhouse's office is full of age, and of things stacked up. On the walls hang half a dozen stuffed fish. Mr. Waterhouse says he just lives to fish. For thirty years he has been head of the biggest fresh-water fishing society in the world. He is the czar of 40,000 English fishermen.

If you think war doesn't affect the average person — well, Mr. Waterhouse has not had time to go fishing since the war started.

On a window ledge is a row of shrapnel and bomb fragments and nose-caps off bombs. These were all picked up right around the plant. "We used to make quite a point of collecting them," Mr. Waterhouse says, "but now they're so common we don't even keep them."

Most of the Waterhouse employees are Home Guardsmen or air-raid wardens in their home suburbs, and all of them take turns as roof spotters at the plant. Mr. Waterhouse takes his turn with them.

He has kept a diary ever since the war started. In it he notes the weather for each day, the number and severity of raids, and the big news of the day. He sees the war as concerned with only one thing — the right to live in a country where you can say what you think and do whatever you damn please.

"Hell, man!" he said. "You couldn't even knock off to go fishing, under Hitler."

Back home I know people have wondered how it could possibly be true that England is getting along with her factory production when Hitler has such a vast air armada and such a little distance to fly it, and when England is so small and congested and easy to hit. I've wondered myself.

Well, for one thing, England is not so small as you might think. It is as far from Lands End, on the south-west, to John O'Groat's, on the north, as it is from New York to Chicago. And crosswise, at the average, England is more than 200 miles wide. You can sprinkle a lot of factories over that much territory, and Britain has sprinkled them.

If they have 2000 factories in Birmingham — which they have — then they have tens of thousands in other places. They are practically everywhere. If Germany knew where they all were, and could send planes over unopposed in the daytime to destroy them, it would take months just to pick them out and blow them up. But with daylight bombing completely whipped, and small spots impossible to find at night, and with even the terrific all-night blitzes getting only a fraction of the factories in a congested area, and with a smooth system of quick repairs to damaged factories — well, Britain has been able to go right on manufacturing through it all.

3. BLITZKISS IN COVENTRY

Coventry,
February, 1941.

Coventry represents to Americans, and to most Englishmen too, the all-out one-night blitz at its worst. Many other cities have been blitzed since then, but Coventry remains the No. 1 example in our minds.

The Coventry blitz occurred on the night of November 14, 1940. I have read a great deal about it, and have seen many pictures of it. Further, I have seen so much hideous damage in London that you could no longer call me an amateur at viewing wreckage. Yet when we drove into Coventry I was horrified.

We walked and drove around Coventry for three hours. And late in the afternoon I realized that I had been saying to myself half out loud, saying it over and over again like a chant: "My God, this is awful!"

The center of Coventry is in ruins. All of the hotels are gone. A big newspaper office is a jumble of wilted presses and linotype machines, with twisted steel girders sagging among them. There are not many public eating places left. You can stand on what used to be a main corner in downtown Coventry, and in three directions see nothing but waste. You can walk down what was a street but now you walk in ankle-deep mud. You would barely recognize it as a street. On each side tractors and cranes and men with blowtorches are untangling and hauling away twisted girders and mingled rubble.

Nobody has been able to put that night of Coventry's into words.

The noise was fiendish. It seemed that the entire city was burning down. They say the final death toll was a little over 500. It seems almost impossible that the loss of life should have been no more than that. For Coventry is a city of a quarter of a million people. That means that only one out of 500 was killed. The only reason many thousands of others didn't lie dead the next morning is that they took to the shelters.

The city had two mass burials, with more than 200 bodies, in each. And such is Coventry's opinion of the Germans that they kept the time of the funerals secret, for fear of a blitz directed at the mourners.

Other dead were buried privately by their families.

Scores of bodies were unidentified. The only way the death of some of the people was known was from the fact that their families never saw them again. I feel certain that they will still be finding bodies in Coventry long after the war is over, when the final removal of tumbled debris is undertaken.

Daylight found Coventry in a daze. I have friends in Birmingham who were here by dawn. As they drove into town they found people leaving the city by any means at hand. My friends say the look of horror in the faces of these people was something they can never forget. Everyone was stunned. You could ask a simple question and they either did not know the answer or would just stare at you. Their minds seemed dead.

What brought people out of this, and back to life again, was two things. One was the visit of the King, who came on the second morning. He came unannounced, and only a few people were around when he arrived, but the word spread quickly. And somehow the realization that the King was there among them startled the people out of their stupor and they were actually able to cheer.

The second thing was the prodding into action by city leaders. An emergency council was immediately formed. A local "Churchill," a man who had never held office, just walked into the breach and started orders flying while others stood by helpless. Loudspeaker trucks and handbills spread the command that Coventry had to be cleaned up. And it was this getting people into action again — even though the action was merely throwing brickbats from one pile onto another — that jerked their spirits back into circulation and started the stream of life flowing once again in Coventry.

We walked through a street that was a no man's land. Utter destruction lay on both sides. One side had been brick houses, the other side a warehouse. Now both sides were just piles of broken brick.

We turned into an alley that had been cleared. A jumble of bricks had been pushed back from the line of the alley, and a little picket fence built around them. The fence was newly painted green.

Back in the alley we found J.B. Shelton. He is living in a brick lean-to about the size of a double bed. It used to be a washhouse, and it has a fireplace at one end.

"J.B." hunted around for a couple of boards and laid them across boxes for us to sit on. The debris we had just passed used to be J.B. Shelton's house and office. In fact, he had owned four houses in a row. They all make one big heap now.

At the edge of the rubble a twisted iron bed sticks out beyond the line of wreckage and gets in the way of the picket fence J.B. is building around his ruins. Since the bed lies in such a way that he can't get it out from the rubble, he is sawing off the protruding ends with a hacksaw so his new picket fence will fit evenly along the line of destruction!

J.B. Shelton is a case. He is not very young, except in enthusiasm. He wears leather leggings, and a funny kind of celluloid collar with no tie, and an old cap. He laughs and talks, and it is hard to get him stopped.

He is a draying contractor, but his life interest is archaeology. In fact, he is Coventry's official archaeologist, although this is merely a job of love and no pay. For years he has been digging up old Roman relics around Coventry. He says the blitz bombs have unearthed wonderful things for him. He is, I believe, the only man in Coventry who is authorized to poke in the ruins anywhere he wants to without getting arrested for looting.

He had a museum of Roman things back there in his alley. It is all shattered and waterlogged now, and many of his prize pieces lie in the mud on the floor. But still he stands there amid the debris and points at an old log and launches into its Roman origins. You'd think you were in a Harvard lecture room instead of standing in an alley in Coventry where you can't see a whole building in any direction.

Finally we got him shunted away from his archaeological talk and onto the night of the disaster.

"Where were you that night?" I asked.

"Where was I?" he said. "I was right here, right here in this alley, running up and down all night long."

And then J.B. Shelton went into action. He made that night almost as clear as if we were living through it.

"My house was already afire, so I just tried to save the stables," he said. His five horses were tied in their stalls in a frame building running along the alley back of the house.

"All night I was running up and down the side of these stables, like this, throwing water on the boards. I got the water out of that open tank there.

"Every once in a while a new place would catch. I'd get it out, and then the hay would be on fire. I'd get it out, and then some sacks of oats would be on fire.

"Around midnight I got the horses all out. They took it fine. I had sacks ready to put over their heads, but only had to do that on one of them. I took them out two at a time so they wouldn't be scared. I got them all out and tied them to trees in that open space back there at the end. Then I had to come back and go after these fires again."

Running up and down and throwing water, with incendiaries and heavy bombs and sparks and timbers falling around him, all night long — all this to save an old clapboard stable that isn't worth fifty dollars!

"Say, it was hot there, mister!" Shelton said. "Sparks were falling just like rain. See all these holes in my old coat? That's where sparks fell on me.

"When I'd hear a big one coming I'd go down like this." And to illustrate he dropped flat on his stomach in the cold mud of the alley.

"The noise was terrific," he said. "All night long the planes were diving right down on top of us. That warehouse there was all afire, and the sparks were a-flying. Say, I'll never see anything like it again. I wouldn't have missed it for anything in the world. Say, it was wonderful!"

And I suppose that if you have the divine gift of looking fully upon life and serenely upon death, such a night really would be wonderful.

Drive out of Coventry today in any direction and on the outskirts of town you'll see vast fields solidly covered with dumped truckloads of brickbats and rubble. As a Coventry friend of mine said, "There are probably more secondhand bricks here today than anywhere else in the world."

While the downtown wreckage is being cleaned up and hauled away, most of Coventry's ruins will have to lie where they are until peace comes. Coventry will not look like a normal city again until many years after the war.

No complete rebuilding is allowed now. But the city is already throwing up little one-story frame buildings with slanting roofs — much like chicken coops — to be used as temporary shops by the merchants who were blasted out.

Coventry is carrying on as best it can. Everybody is back at work, but few people are living normally. A good portion of the population are living in single rooms salvaged from shattered homes.

For three days after the blitz all of Coventry lived on sandwiches carried around in mobile canteens. After that, communal kitchens were set up to provide hot food. Rationing was discontinued, but has now been resumed.

There is plenty of food in the shops now, but the shops are so few that there are always long lines of people waiting to get in.

Once more the beautiful girls of Coventry (and I mean beautiful) grace the streets. And best of all, the dog races have started again. The profits go to the relief of Coventry's bomb victims.

If you get a chance to see the short film, "This Is Britain," which is now showing in America, I hope you'll go. And when you do, look for a Coventry woman named Pearl Hyde. She makes a little speech in the film.

Well, I know Pearl Hyde. She is one of Coventry's greatest heroines. She has just been decorated with the Order of the British Empire for her bravery.

Hers was not just a frenzied gallantry of the moment. It was a coolness and tirelessness that lasted ten days and nights on end, almost without sleep.

Pearl Hyde is head of the Coventry branch of the Women's Voluntary Services. It was Pearl Hyde who fed and clothed and cheered and really saved the people of Coventry after the blitz. For more than a week she plowed around in the ashes of Coventry, wearing policeman's pants. She never took off her clothes. She was so black they could hardly tell her from a Negro.

Her Women's Voluntary Services headquarters was bombed out, so she and her women moved across the street. Her own home was blown up, and even today she still sleeps in the police station.

Pearl Hyde is a huge woman, tall and massive. Her black hair is cut in a boyish bob. And she has personality that sparkles with power and good nature. She is much better looking than in the film. And she is laughing all the time.

She was just ready to dash off somewhere when I went in to see her, but she tarried a few minutes to tell me how good the Americans had been with donations. She talked past her time. Suddenly she looked at her watch and jumped up in a great rush. I held out my hand by way of good-bye, but instead of shaking hands Pearl Hyde grabbed my frail shoulders in her great hands and said: "Here's a kiss for America." And she smacked me a big one right on the face.

As little loath as I am to be embraced by the feminine gender any time, any place, I was rendered stone dumb by this sudden attack. I stood there speechless and blushing as Heroine Hyde strode away with great long steps and all her fellow women workers stood laughing with delight.

And so, when one of these days I step into a homeward-bound plane I will carry as souvenirs of this shattered city a couple of small pieces of broken tile, a mental picture of destruction that can never be erased, and last but best — a large, ample Coventry blitzkiss.

4. NOTES ON THE CUFF

Warwick,
March, 1941

This is a small and ancient city on the banks of the River Avon. It is just ten miles from Stratford-on-Avon, the immortal home of Shakespeare.

I ducked in here for a week-end in the hope of writing some ageless literature while under the spell of Shakespeare. But the hotel thought we were still living in The Bard's time, and consequently I spent the weekend in bed with a hot-water bottle. If you mention the word heat around here they report you to the police as a suspicious character.

After breakfast I fled outdoors and walked around town for an hour just to get warmed up. Motor travellers were passing through town, and within ten minutes two cars pulled alongside me to ask directions. One driver wanted to know how to get to Stratford. The other asked the way to Kenilworth. I didn't know, so I merely replied, "Brother, I've even forgotten the way to New York." In each case the motorist drove quickly on, looking back as though he thought I was touched in the head, and possibly even subversive.

Being too cold to think, I thought I would just put down a few tag ends of the last few weeks, which have stuck in my mind.

84

For one thing, here is a little item about the old tradition that Scotsmen are so tight. Well, back in November the government sent out a frantic call for all citizens to turn in binoculars, as they were needed in the armed forces. You could either donate, lend or sell them to the government. And up to date the proportion of binoculars donated outright to the government is three times as great in Scotland as in England!

The three most popular entertainers who ever visited Glasgow are Harry Lauder, John McCormack and Gene Autry.

Of the things I brought with me from America, the wisest of all was a pair of galoshes. I have worn them almost constantly for the past month, and I think I would be dead without them. For some reason they don't have galoshes in England. I'll bet thirty people have commented on my pair and said they wished they could get some.

English hotels all start their day at noon. Consequently it is possible — and has actually happened to me — to stay only one night at a hotel and yet be forced to pay for two nights.

There is a saying all over England that the safest place to be during a raid is in a church spire, and I am beginning to believe it. I have seen dozens of wrecked churches but I don't remember one whose steeple wasn't still standing.

One funny thing about blitzed cities — you always see, either lying around or stuck on a pole by some jocular workman, a naked wax dummy from a store window. There was one in Coventry on top of a steel post stuck in a pile of jumbled brick right in the center of town. In another town I saw a dummy propped up on the sidewalk, and a local man said they had found the dummy's foot two blocks away.

I haven't heard a warning siren since leaving London, but people tell me the sirens sound exactly the same all over Britain.

A very friendly lady who has donated her car and her driving services to the government drove me down here from Birmingham. There are thousands of such women in Britain. This particular one was a Mrs. Matty, and I mention it because she has a sister named Mrs. James Cruse who lives in Denver.

In Britain you never hear the war of 1914-18 spoken of as the World War. They always say "the last war."

The other day a newspaper proposed that we call the last one "German War 1, and this one German War 2, and just keep on numbering them in the future until we run out of numbers."

England likes to tell jokes on the regimented minds of its civil-service employees. They say this one is true: In order to get onto an R.A.F. station you have to have a special pass, which is usually a small slip of pink paper. So the other day a girl of the Women's Auxiliary Air Force received an order from Whitehall which said, "Report to R.A.F. station such-and-such at 10 a.m. and show your pink form."

If it weren't for the soldiers on the streets and the one lump of sugar for your coffee, it would be hard to realize a war was on when you visit many of England's small cities and towns which have never known the crunch of a bomb.

In the provinces, policemen still wear fore-and-aft hats instead of steel helmets.

A lady from America writes and wants to know if I am wearing a correspondent's uniform. The answer is no. The only ones who wear uniforms are those accredited to the army. There are only a few of these.

As for me, I feel silly enough carrying a tin hat and a gas mask around the provinces, let alone appearing in a uniform.

PART IX: YOU HAVENT SEEN ANYTHING

1. THE WAR IN WALES

Cardiff,
March, 1941.

The very first sight that greets you as you walk out of the railroad station in Cardiff is the city's big municipal stadium. It sits quite alone, surrounded by a grassy park. It is like some of the fine stadiums at home, with a great steel-trussed grandstand, roofed over. It cost a lot of money, and the people of Cardiff have packed it on big soccer and rugby days.

But Cardiff should have known better than to erect this deadly war machine right out in the open, for you can't fool Hitler. He knows all about the airplanes and tanks and battleships they've been building out there on the cricket field. And so he has blown their stadium all to hell.

Outside of that, you don't see much bomb damage around Cardiff. If you were to set out deliberately on a "damage tour" you could pick out quite a total of wrecked houses and burned stores; but if you are just wandering around like a tourist the bomb wreckage doesn't stare you in the face around every corner.

The sizes of British cities are always amazing me. Cardiff, for instance, is a city of a quarter of a million people. And did you ever hear of Newport? I'm sure I never did. Well, it's only ten miles from Cardiff, and its population is 100,000.

Wales, as you know, forms the west central part of Britain. It is noted for its coal mines, and somewhat for the bad condition of its miners. And Wales is mountainous. To my surprise I have found that there are mountains on this island rising as high as 3000 to 4000 feet, but the mountainous sections are thinly populated. The bulk of Wales's population of more than two million is settled along the southern coast.

The Welsh people look and dress very much the same as Americans. They are noted as singers, but I've not heard anybody singing in Cardiff.

You see an amazing number of bicycles here. Late in the evening, when people are on their way home from work, you can hardly cross the street for the bicycles.

I had supposed that Cardiff was a grimy, smoky city, bearing the marks of the coal-mining industry. To my amazement, it turned out to be light and clean, much more so than most English cities. The streets are wide, there are vast parks and lovely buildings, and as you go around you pick up a feeling that Cardiff has everything in hand.

Cardiff is full of defenses. More street obstructions are noticeable here than in most of the places I've visited. Every city seems to have its own special type of street barricade with which to stop the German invaders if they come. Public shelters are different in Cardiff, too. Everywhere else the street shelters are made of a tan-colored brick, but in Cardiff most of them are concrete.

There is very little public sheltering in basements here. The big street shelters are preferred. In the residential sections these shelters are built right in the middle of the street. In case the bombing gets hot, people have only to run out their front doors and halfway across the street.

I ran into something in Cardiff I had not seen in any other city — automobiles driven by coal gas. The point is that gasoline is rationed, and coal gas isn't.

A huge canvas bag is installed on the roof of the car, and surrounded with a railing. It looks like about five layers of featherbed. The only change in the motor that's necessary is a new top to the carburetor.

It's all right as a makeshift, but not too satisfactory. For one thing, it costs $120 to equip the car for coal gas. Then you don't get as much power as with gasoline. And that big bag has a terrific wind resistance. When the gas gets low the bag flops around in the breeze. Also, if there is a heavy snow or rain, the weight presses down on the bag and forces gas into the carburetor too fast, making the engine choke and backfire.

And worst of all, you look silly as hell driving down the street with this balloon on top of you.

The WVS (Women's Voluntary Services) has done excellent work in Cardiff, as it has everywhere else.

I somehow managed to get myself into the good graces of the WVS commander for all Wales. She turned out to be a beautiful, cultured girl only two years out of a university. When I asked her how one so young had risen so high, she said it was a mystery to her too. Her name is typically Welsh — Eirwen Owen. She can even make a speech in Welsh if she has to. She has some 8000 women under her, and she handles it all with the utmost calm.

The WVS was anxious for me to know how much they appreciated the gifts sent from America. They said they didn't know how they would have clothed all the bombed-out people and poor evacuees who have come from other sections if it hadn't been for the American gifts.

We went around to one of their distributing sections, where half a dozen women in green smocks were sorting out and repacking huge boxes of stuff from America. It has been quite an education for them. They read on the bills of lading such unknown items — to them — as slickers, Mackinaws, and gum boots. They had never heard of these things by these names. They open the big wooden boxes as though they were Christmas packages — to see what a Mackinaw is. In most cases they are immensely pleased; but one thing did stop them — union suits. They had never heard of union suits. Over here nobody ever saw underwear all in one piece before. In fact, when they went to distribute them, lots of old-fashioned Welsh people refused to take them.

And while we're on the subject of American gifts, maybe the merchants of San Francisco would like to know that some of those boxes of elaborate mechanical erector sets they sent over are now in Wales. They got here too late for Christmas, but they're being distributed now by the women of the WVS, who think they're the most wonderful things they ever saw.

Once in a while German bombers come over Cardiff and drop propaganda leaflets. The last time they did it the pamphlets were a translation of one of Hitler's speeches. The people of Cardiff consider this such a great joke they collect them as souvenirs to keep after the war, and they are actually peddled around for a shilling apiece.

Cardiff has 600 Belgian refugees. And to their eternal discredit, they are making asses of themselves — demanding, complaining, pestering. They are the crankiest people in a jam that Cardiff has ever had to deal with.

I have been riding around Wales with a gentle Welshman by the name of Eames whose wife is a first cousin of Chief Justice Hughes. Which would make it a small world after all if I only happened to know Chief Justice Hughes.

2. MINER

Ebbw Vale,
March, 1941

This is a coal-mining town of about 30,000 people in the hills of Monmouthshire, near the border of Wales.

The altitude is only 900 feet here, but the hills roll in long, vast ridges, and there are no trees; the snow lies deep on the ground, whereas down on the coast it has all melted. You have a feeling of great height here. All day long I had to pinch myself to realize I was not somewhere in the Rockies, above timberline.

The coal miners in and near Wales have had tough going since the last war. They are among Britain's neediest people. And unlike the rest of Britain, unlike most of the warring populations, the present conflict hasn't done their employment much good.

The reason lies in transportation. The railroads are tied up hauling munitions, and they haul only such coal as is necessary. There's no real coal shortage in England, but nobody has any more than just enough. And there's no use digging coal if you can't haul it away and sell it. Consequently the mines aren't working in any frenzy. The loss of French markets was a blow too.

Ebbw Vale happens to be very prosperous at the moment, due to local manufacturing which uses coal, but it is rather the exception. Western Wales is still in the lower brackets of depression, and a good part of its working population has gone to great factory centers such as Birmingham and Manchester, seeking work.

I came to Ebbw Vale to see how close the war has come to the average family over here in the hills. My "average man" turned out to be Henry Powell. He lives in a two-story brick-row house on a sloping street. Children were sliding down the street on sleds.

Henry Powell is seventy-one, and he is well preserved. He has spent fifty years underground and it hasn't hurt him. He retired from coal-digging a couple of years ago, on a small pension, but is back at work again now, for he wanted to do a little something in the war. They have put him to cutting down timber supports in unused mine tunnels.

Henry Powell has a big family. There are eight in his house. His sister lives next door, and there are half a dozen in her house. They are all mixed up — children, nieces, nephews, grandchildren and in-laws.

Mr. Powell owns his home. He started buying it when it was brand-new, and moved into it the year after I was born, which was 39 years ago.

Mrs. Powell is dead now. Two of Mr. Powell's sons were in the World War and one of them was gassed. Some of his grandsons are already in the Home Guard, awaiting their call-ups for the regular army.

Just before Mr. Powell quit the deep pits two years ago there were three generations of his family working side by side in the pits — himself, three sons and three grandsons.

Mr. Powell feels that he has done pretty well for a miner. He has bought his house, raised a big family, taken care of his relatives, kept himself respectable, and has nothing to regret. His home is comfortably and nicely furnished, and he himself is as neat and clean as a whistle.

He has had only two holidays in his life. (Over here when they say holiday they mean three or four weeks off in which to take a long trip.) He has been to London a couple of times.

He doesn't smoke, but for fifty years he has stopped for two pints of beer on his way home from work every evening.

About the only way the Powells are directly affected by the war is through the rationing of food. But they don't suffer for anything. There are some shelters in Ebbw Vale, but the Powells have never been in them. All in all, life is not a great deal different for them from what it was in peacetime, and they themselves, in truth, are not much different from Americans.

3. NO MAN'S LAND

Bristol,
March, 1941.

It was midafternoon when I got off the train. We had come through the long tunnel under Bristol Channel, and the compartment had been full of smoke. So I checked in at a hotel and went to my room to wash off the soot.

It had been more than three weeks since I had heard a siren, a bomb or a gun. After a lull like that, you actually get out of practice. You drop your protective armor of expectancy. Thus it was that I was standing there all relaxed in a quiet hotel room, washing my hands, when all of a sudden there was the damnedest explosion I ever heard. It shook the windows, and made the curtains puff, and to say that it shook me would be a vast understatement of fact.

My first conclusion was that it was a sneak daytime raider, but still it hadn't sounded just like a bomb. So I sat down and tried to think. I finally figured out that it must be dynamiters, blasting some unsafe bombed walls just back of the hotel. And that's what it was.

After my strength came back I called up some people to whom I had a note, and arranged to meet them.

"Gee whiz," I said when we got together, "Bristol has certainly been knocked around. I didn't know Bristol had had it this bad."

"Why," they said, "you haven't seen anything. Come on."

So we taxied to a certain corner where the street was blocked, and then got out and walked. It was the worst day I have seen this winter. There was a somber black rain that was nearly sleet, and a piercing wind that cut through any kind of clothes.

And so, bent against the storm, we walked. Walked through streets where on Saturday nights a hundred thousand people used to mill up and down, but where today all was silent. For this part is now closed to the public; you can enter only with credentials. It is a No Man's Land.

This part of Bristol is just as bare and ruined and destroyed as any 1918 village in France that we used to see in pictures. In fact, it looks exactly like those pictures. Only a few walls are left standing. There is such an incongruous maze of hanging, twisted girders as I have never seen elsewhere. Tearing it all apart and hauling it away will surely be a greater job than building it in the first place.

Drive around Bristol, and all over the city you will find whole blocks knocked down and burned up. And there is a general scattered devastation that is staggering if you add it up.

My friends and I wandered like children back and forth amid this strange land that used to be. I said almost nothing, for what was there to say? I had never known that anything could actually be like this.

In the midst of our wanderings I saw a familiar figure coming toward us. He was walking with a policeman down the middle of what had been a street, and he was huddled deep in his coat against the bitter rain. I knew the man well, yet so ghostly was the setting, and so strange this place we inhabited, that I could not believe a human acquaintance of mine could be there too, in the flesh, on such a weird, mystic day.

It was Gault Macgowan of the New York Sun. Neither of us knew the other was in Bristol. I have not seen him since to talk it over, but I believe he must have had the same strange feeling about me. For he came up and looked at me for a long time, in a puzzled way, before he spoke. We said a few words of surprise, and then walked on again in opposite directions, on through a kind of world I hope America never sees.

I truly believe that if it were possible for you to come to Bristol directly from America, arriving blindfolded so you could not accustom yourself gradually by seeing lesser damage as you drove along, and let me lead you to this vast blocked-off graveyard in Bristol and then suddenly snatch off the blindfold and let the fury of the scene engulf you all at once — I truly believe there is not one person out of ten, man or woman, who would not stand there with tears in his eyes, and his head bowed in anguish and despair.

In Bristol I met a man who is a "reader" in imperial history at the University of Bristol. The great hall of the university, with its lovely walls paneled in oak, stands just outside the professor's window, or rather did stand there before the fire bombs gutted it.

My history professor says the hall was the most beautiful thing he had ever seen. To him its loss was the worst of all the blows that have befallen Bristol. My professor is blind, but just the same he can see these beautiful things that are now gone.

He invited me to come out to his apartment after dinner. His name is Charles MacInnis, and there's nothing professorish about him at all. He said he couldn't offer me anything to drink except whisky, beer and wine. I told him not to worry, that we had to put up with these hardships in wartime.

He insisted on sending a taxi for me, because it is hard to get taxis at night in Bristol. The sirens sounded just before the taxi came. The driver took me out in a hurry, for he was on roof-spotting duty at his garage and he had to get right back. He wouldn't have come at all if the sirens had sounded before he started. He said he'd return for me at ten-thirty if the all clear had sounded. If it hadn't, I would just have to wait.

Mr. MacInnis is a Canadian, from Calgary. He has always been blind.

Once he took a crack at newspaper work in Calgary. "But because I was blind they thought I was religious," he said, "so they put me on the church notices. That's all the newspaper work I ever did."

In 1915 he finished school in Canada and came on to Oxford. When he finished there, the University of Bristol offered him a job. He has been here ever since. He is one of Bristol's most active citizens. He has written a book about Bristol, and he gave me a copy of it. He married a Bristol girl, and they have a twelve-year-old boy who has now been evacuated to the country with his grandparents.

The MacInnises have a nice six-room apartment with a center hallway, a library, and a big sitting room at one end. We went into the sitting room, and in the middle of the floor there stood a table with nine wooden pins on it and a stick raised above, from which hung a wooden ball on a string.

"Have you ever played table skittles?" Mr. MacInnis asked.

"I never even heard of it," I said.

"Then you had better learn," he said. "That's what they play in the pubs around here. Everybody plays it."

So we played, and Mrs. MacInnis won both games.

"I like this game because it isn't intellectual," the professor said.

The all clear sounded as we were playing the second game.

"Do you have a shelter in the basement?" I asked.

"There is one," Mr. MacInnis said, "but we've never been down."

"Not even during those terrible all-night blitzes?"

"Not even then," he said. "What's the use? You might get buried. We never stir from the apartment. You sort of get used to it."

"How do your dogs take it?" I asked. They have two beautiful dogs, a Samoyed and a cocker.

Mr. MacInnis laughed. "They don't get frightened," he said. "In fact, they don't seem to mind it at all, except for screaming bombs. One of those screamers sounds like a cat howling, you know, and the dogs set up an awful howl."

The basement shelter has a gas-proof room for the dogs, in case gas ever comes.

"I don't want you to think I'm impertinent," I said, "but can you describe to me what a blind man's conception is of the damage to Bristol?"

"Well," Mr. MacInnis said, "I'm sensitive to light, and when I walk down the street I suddenly realize there is light at my side and I know I am passing a building that isn't there any more. I see it as piles of brick, partly standing walls, charred timbers and twisted girders."

And I realized that although he was using the same words of description that I use, there was no possible way for him to tell me what he sees in his mind, because piles of brick and charred timbers are only words to him. He has never seen any.

Mr. MacInnis is a hard worker. He does voluntary work day and night. He has a job that might best be described as that of a morale-keeper-up for the blitzed and homeless of Bristol. He makes speeches, organizes entertainments, helps people find homes, and gets better things for the shelters. Everyone I met was full of praise for him.

He has lots of humor — a sort of sardonic humor. He thinks the funniest war story is one that happened right at the university, and he heard it himself. It seems that Kings College, a big medical school in London, decided to evacuate to Bristol. All the professors arrived and held their first meeting on the morning after Bristol had experienced one of its worst blitzes and many scores of people lay dead.

"The meeting was very serious and businesslike," Mr. MacInnis said. "The professors were doubtful whether they could carry on normal instructions here because transportation from London was not so good and the new school was not properly equipped with corpses!"

The doorbell rang. The all clear having sounded, our taxi driver was back on the dot. Mr. MacInnis ran ahead of me down two flights of stairs and out the front door into the dark street to the taxi. And as I groped my way behind him, it dawned on me that this vile blackout which is scourging England today has no terrors at all for a man who is blind. As the philosophers would say, there is recompense in everything.

4. LONGSHORE PUB

Shirehampton,
March, 1941.

Last night I decided to do a little pub-crawling, to see if I could dig up a piece of conversation among some longshoremen.

I have always thought of longshoremen as hard guys, quick to suspect an outsider. So I sidled up to the bar sort of timidly. But these longshoremen were so suspicious that before two minutes had passed I had the life history of the fellow next to me, voluntarily. The problem wasn't getting him started, it was getting him stopped.

His name was "Nobby" Clark. In fact, all the Clarks in these parts are called Nobby. This special Nobby lost a leg in the last war. His brother was killed in France. His two sons are in the forces now. His sister and a niece were killed by a bomb last fall. And now his own house has been blown up, and he and his wife are living with friends.

"But Hitler won't get me," Nobby says. "I'm too tough and too lucky. Here, wait a minute, a stranger can't pay for his own here, and anyway this is my birthday. Here's to ol' Hitler, bad luck to 'im!"

Well, that was a good start, so then we got to talking to Tom Woolacombe and his brother-in-law. They are dock workers too.

The brother-in-law's left arm was in a plaster cast. It seems he and another fellow were sitting in front of their fireplace one night, and everything was peaceful and quiet, and no raid was on, and all of a sudden the whole side of the house, fireplace and all, leaped out and fell on them.

The reason for this odd behavior on the part of the house was that a time bomb had buried itself in the ground just outside, one night earlier, and nobody knew about it till it went off. The boys said they sure were surprised.

After a while Tom suggested that we walk up to his place, which was just a couple of blocks. So we got two bottles of beer for his wife and walked home in the moonlight. Mrs. Woolacombe was a little disconcerted to see Tom home so early, and with a stranger too, and she obviously wasn't any too pleased about it. But after we talked a while everything was all right.

The Woolacombes, to be blunt about it, have had a bellyful of this war. As Mrs. Woolacombe puts it, "I'm proper fed up. Bombs, bombs, bombs, all the time."

You're afraid to go anywhere. You get so jumpy you hate everything. Sitting out there in that lousy Anderson shelter night after night gets on your nerves. And what's the use to plant vegetables in your back yard? The bombs are just as liable to come along and blow them up.

Yes, the Woolacombes are proper fed up.

Tom has steady work unloading ships. He is 57. He says he makes just enough to get by. They live pretty well, but there is nothing left over on payday. They rent their two-story six-room house for $2.75 a week, which they consider high.

Their two sons are in the army. So is their married daughter's husband. Another daughter, Alice, whose husband has been killed, lives with them.

Alice has a little boy three years old, and I noticed that he kept walking around saying to himself, "War's over. War's over."

"What's he saying that for?" I asked his mother.

"Well," she said, "several weeks ago he wanted something, I forget what, and I told him he couldn't have it till the war was over. Ever since he has been saying 'War's over' to himself all the time."

It sounds like using the Coue system on the war.

There are two more Woolacombe girls. Eileen, who is sixteen, sells tickets at a movie theater. Violet, who is twenty, works in a munitions factory.

The Woolacombes have had an incendiary bomb through their roof. This was during a heavy raid, and they were all in the backyard shelter. Things got a little quiet, so Alice stuck her head out to see what was what. And it looked as if the whole world was afire. So they all jumped out and ran to the house, and some neighbors and wardens came running too. They finally got the incendiary put out. All their sand was frozen solid, so they had to use ashes out of the grate. The fire burned up all the clothes in a corner closet. They've got this room closed off now, and aren't using it.

After a while we went back to the pub and sat around talking with a lot of longshoremen. It is the custom here for men to eat an early supper at home and then go to the pub and sit from seven till ten, when the pubs dose.

The men were mostly middle-aged and there was no loud talk or singing, such as you find in so many pubs on these wartime nights.

These longshoremen carried the bitterest feeling about the war that I've run onto yet. "This ain't war," they say. "This is just plain murder, bombing our homes and women and children like this." If I heard that once, I heard it twenty times.

These men are mostly veterans of the last war and they still have an idea that wars should be fought on the battlefield. As you can see, they are very old-fashioned and don't understand the New World Order.

5. BACK TO LONDON

London,
March, 1941.

And so back to the big city.

The returned sojourner can see changes in London after being gone for a month. Not much physical change, of course, for the bombings were light during most of my absence. But there is more sugar, more chocolate, more cigarettes. In a restaurant the waiter brought four lumps of sugar and whispered, "Two for your first cup, two for your second." Of course he was angling for a bigger tip, and he angled well.

There are now plenty of chocolates in the shops, whereas chocolates were close to being extinct right after the holidays.

There has never been a real shortage of cigarettes, but there has been a scarcity of various brands. When I first came to England I shopped around among the English cigarettes to see what most closely resembled the American kind. I finally lit on one called Wix. Well, the day I left London for the north I went to fifteen tobacco shops and succeeded in collecting only five packs of Wix. Yet on my return when I went Wix-hunting again the first two tobacconists sold me a carton each.

While there are more cigarettes and sugar and chocolates, there is less meat. For several nights now they say Simpson's has been without its famous roast beef. My hotel has no steaks or chops. This is a temporary shortage, possibly due to transportation trouble, but it is becoming more habitual all over London.

There seems to be more food and a greater variety of it everywhere in the provinces than in London. The smaller the town the more food there is. The supply of sugar and eggs is practically normal in the smaller places.

The Food Ministry has announced a general all-around tightening of the British belt, and I think it's a good thing. For an island that imports so much and has such vulnerable sea lanes, England has been eating too much. As a matter of fact, the Food Ministry is several months behind the people. They have been quite willing for a long time to have their belts tightened.

Furthermore, the picture of rich people eating grandiosely in restaurants while the poor theoretically go hungry is rapidly becoming a hallucination. You still pay exorbitantly at the big hotels, and you get all the overabundance of silverware and yessirs and delay that seems to be fashionable, but when you come to sum up what you've had to eat you could have fared better in somebody's home.

And speaking of food, you may remember that a while back I said the only thing I missed over here was enough sugar. That must have put ideas into people's heads, for I have already received two one-pound boxes of sugar from readers in America. And I hear that more is on the way.

One box was sent by Mr. and Mrs. Dick Petticrew of East Lansing, Michigan, whom I don't know. On the customs declaration which accompanied the package they had to indicate to whom it should be delivered if I couldn't be found. So the Petticrews wrote "Winston Churchill."

Scotland has become a new national home for the Poles who got away after the German occupation. There are many thousands of Poles in Scotland now, and most of them are in the army. They get along well with the Scots.

They are fine soldiers. Nobody in this war is fighting with more burning fire in the soul than the Poles. I have yet to hear a word about them that wasn't in praise. No German will ever get mercy from a Pole on this island.

The other day I saw a question sent from America asking what people in theaters did when an air-raid warning sounded. Well, I can tell you.

Having a touch of the heebie-jeebies, I decided to go to a movie. The picture was "Dulcy," and everybody thought it was swell. The theater was a huge one in Leicester Square, and it was packed. In the middle of the picture the film stopped and a sign was flashed on the screen. It said the sirens had just sounded and that anyone who wished could leave and go to the public shelters across the street. The picture was then resumed.

Not a soul in that whole theater stirred.

Afterward another sign flashed, saying the all clear had sounded.

People simply don't pay attention to daytime warnings any more. Even my own faint heart ceased long since to do even a slight dervish when the sirens moan.

I think I have enough official British credentials in my wallet to get me out of anything, up to and including assassination. Yet in all my recent travels I have been called upon to show them only twice.

Both cases were ridiculous. Once it was a matter of a nosey hotel clerk in Wales. The other instance was in the peaceful Cotswold Hills of Gloucestershire. There I had to identify myself in a big way before being allowed to see a communal dining room for evacuees. You could have sat Hitler down there for a meal and he wouldn't have found out anything.

That's one trouble with war — the farther you are from it the sillier the people get.

In most of Great Britain they are too busy to fuss-budget with red tape. I have been amazed at the utter freedom in England today. People come and go, brag and criticize, talk and listen. It is remarkable and admirable.

On gun stations, at flying fields, in pubs or on trains, I have never run into anybody who seemed suspicious or secretive. The average Englishman just can't conceive of there being a fifth column in this country, and as a general premise I think he is right.

In fact, in wartime England today I believe you can nose around with less bogeyman interference than you can in America.

In spite of being accepted everywhere over here on friendly and intimate terms, I am an American and therefore an alien, and all the alien laws apply to me. For example, it is against the law for me to have a guidebook now without a permit. I am a criminal if I carry the famous Baedeker guidebook of Great Britain, even though the damned thing is printed in Leipzig and the Germans have all the copies they want.

It is a little shaming somehow to be considered an alien, when I speak the same language and am on the same side of the fence. In fact, I don't like it, and I said so to an English newspaper friend of mine. But his answer stopped me cold. He said:

"Well, I worked in New York on the Sun for eight years, and I was an alien over there!"

I hadn't thought of that.

Road signs have been taken down all over England, in case of invasion. The names of towns on public and private signs have been painted over with black paint. The result is that the average Englishman trying to drive even a little way from home gets lost and has to stop and inquire the way about every two miles.

It is against the law to leave a car that could be driven away by the Germans. You have to immobilize your car when you leave it, even though you might be walking only fifty feet away to ask a policeman for directions. In daytime, just locking the doors and taking the key counts as immobilization, but at night you have to take out some vital part, such as the distributor.

Most cars over here are small ones, from 8 to 15 horsepower. No new cars at all are being manufactured for sale. The price of second-hand cars is shooting up, because the army is taking all it can get.

If you wreck your car badly it is almost impossible to get repairs, due to the control of materials and the shortage of civilian mechanics. Many garages and gas stations are closed. A great many garage men have gone into the tank corps. These tank corps men wear the regular brown uniform, the same as the rest of the army, but they have a blue cloth cap, like a beret, which drops over one ear, making them look very cocky and tough.

During the past month I have traveled about 1500 miles by train and 500 by car, and except for small things the travel service was excellent. I have been on twelve different trains, and except for the week-end we got caught in a Yorkshire blizzard I've never been more than half an hour late in reaching my destination.

In the latter part of my travels, after getting the hang of things, I rode third-class all the time. It's about one-third cheaper, and the only difference is that the seats are just a shade nicer in first class and you sit with officers instead of soldiers. Frequently there are first- and third-class compartments in the same car.

The railroads get a lot of criticism, but I think they are doing wonderfully. They have not been taken over by the government.

Occasionally a section of track will be blown to extinction. The railroads have a time limit on themselves of ten hours, I believe it is, no matter how big the crater or how twisted the wreckage, in which to have trains moving again across the bombed spot.

And the way these trains blast along through the night, with no lights, gives you the shivers. One road has just raised its wartime speed limit from sixty miles an hour to seventy-five.

There is one thing about the British railroads that I haven't figured out yet. You'll get on a train that is the dinkiest local you ever saw, stopping at every crossroads, taking hours to go a few miles. Then all of a sudden, halfway to where you're going, the thing mysteriously becomes a highball express and makes the last half of the trip going like the wind, roaring through cities without even stopping.

I suppose it's just a change of pace to fool Hitler.

PART X: BOMBS DO THE DAMNEDEST THINGS

1. "SHUT UP, THEY'LL HEAR YOU!"

London,
March, 1941.

I suppose every person in England who has had a bomb within a block of him has his own freak bomb story to tell. Bombs seem to do the damnedest things. Every raid brings a flock of incidents as miraculous as the old one about the tornado blowing a straw through a tree.

Most of the unusual bomb stories have to do with escapes. Air Raid Precautions men say there are more freakish escapes than freakish deaths. For example, one bomb on a recent night came right through the roof of a building and smack into a pub full of men sitting there drinking beer. It blew the place all to pieces, killed some people in a house across the street — and hurt no one in the pub.

In another case, a bomb glanced off a roof and landed in the open. It apparently had a delayed fuse. Two policemen went up to inspect it, and it went off. No trace ever was found of one policeman, but the other one — well, the blast blew his tin hat onto the roof of a five-story building, and blew all the buttons off his coat, but he wasn't hurt.

In Stepney a policeman was doing roof-spotting duty on top of a seven-story building. A bomb hit the building and blew the policeman off the roof. He fell seven stories, and landed on concrete. He went to work as usual the next day.

In my room I have a circular lead nosepiece from a German bomb. It is about half as big as a saucer, and must weigh two pounds. It came screaming into the apartment of a friend of mine one night, and this friend gave it to me. It arrived in his place through a window, flying horizontally and spinning furiously. It hit a wall, and it was spinning so fast it circled three walls of the room, just like a hippodrome motorcycle racer who rides against the vertical wall of a bowl. But the astounding thing is that in its mad rush this heavy disk raced right across the glass doors of a built-in china closet in one corner and never even cracked the glass.

One surprising thing about bomb explosions is that the suction toward the explosion is almost as great as the blast away from it. That's because the explosion creates a vacuum, and then as air rushes back into the vacuum it does so with just about the same hideous force with which it rushed away. Because of that you'll see wreckage from the same bomb hurled in opposite directions. Say a bomb lands in a street. On one side it may blow a house inward, but on the other side the whole front of a house may be sucked out. I know one case where the suction of a bomb pulled a rug off the floor right from underneath two tables and a piano, and left them standing just as they were.

And then there is the story — my man says he saw it — of a skilletful of frying fish being blown off a stove in one house and landing upright on a stove in a house four doors away. My man does go so far as to admit that the skillet lost its contents on the way.

I believe all those stories. It would be hard to tell me a bomb story I wouldn't believe. But here's one even I must take with a grain of salt:

A gentle lady of culture and means was sitting in front of a fireplace on the ground floor of her home one evening. Her housemaid, having finished her work, was sitting in her little attic bedroom on the fourth floor. A bomb came through the roof, plunged through four successive stories, and exploded in the basement. When it was all over the gentle lady was sitting in her maid's attic rocking-chair and the maid was sitting downstairs in front of the fireplace.

Both were unhurt, of course. And both quite unruffled, you may be sure.

Maybe lightning never strikes twice in the same place, but bombs do. I could show you a narrow brick-row house in London that has been hit five times, yet not another house in the block has been touched. Also, I know cases where a bomb has fallen through the darkness for four miles and landed in the center of a crater blown by a previous bomb.

There is an odd belief in London that corner buildings attract bombs. It doesn't seem reasonable, yet I have seen scores of corner places blown down, with everything else all around them untouched. At Coventry I saw one street corner where four separate bombs had taken out the four corner houses.

On the other hand, just two blocks from my hotel there is a small crater in the middle of a street intersection, where a traffic cop would- normally be standing, and none of the corner buildings has been touched.

Those who hold with the corner theory think air currents, caused by the funneling of air through the streets, force a bomb to deviate just a little at the last second. I can't see it.

A Fleet Street friend of mine went out one night and got himself tight. He managed to drive his car home through the blackout, but the entrance of his garage was narrow and, being three and a half sheets in the wind, he decided just to leave the car out in the street. During the night his garage was demolished.

I have been told of a woman in a suburb who thought she heard a knock at the door. As she opened it a small bomb came sailing through, kerplunk onto the living-room floor. The lady gave a yell and dashed out the door. About three seconds later she saw her house fly into a million pieces.

One of my best friends here is an American who has a horror of crossing a street during the blackout. He has lived here several years and knows hundreds of people. Two close friends of his were killed by autos in the blackout, yet he has never known anyone, even casually, who was killed by a bomb.

Friends are always telling me about shrapnel falling around them. I have been out in the streets a lot at night but I've heard only one piece of shrapnel fall.

I do know, however, that if you're out when the guns are firing pretty heavily you find yourself edging over toward the inside of the sidewalk, against the building walls. No matter how hard you pull yourself out toward the curb, you discover you're still walking along close to the buildings.

I have a friend who was driving into town one night when a piece of shrapnel hit the street, just missing the car. But it bounced so hard it came back up through his fender from underneath and left a big hole.

Another funny thing about raids — when you hear planes overhead you have a feeling that you must be very quiet or the German pilots will hear you. If I'm in my room I unconsciously stop typing for fear of making a noise and attracting the bomber's attention. Often, while planes are overhead, you can hear people down in the street in the dark yelling for taxis at the top of their lungs. I always feel like opening a window and yelling, "Shut up, you fools, they'll hear you!"

Some people seem to attract exciting incidents as though they were magnets. George Lait hadn't been here a week till he had been blown off the seat of a car, had put out incendiaries that came through his roof, and had seen shrapnel smack the sidewalk within three feet of him.

But me — the nearest I have been to drama was one night when we had seven incendiaries on the roof of our hotel and a bomb around the corner, and that happened to be the night I was visiting an antiaircraft gun station miles away! It's probably just as well. Maybe I wasn't cut out to be a hero anyhow.

2. GERMANS, ARISE AND FLEE

London,
March, 1941.

Tex Bradford walked into my room at seven-thirty in the evening and said he had only a few minutes. He took off his coat and threw it on the bed, and asked if he could wash up. He left at two-thirty the next morning and hadn't washed up yet.

Tex is one of the many Americans over here serving with the Canadian Army. He's a good old boy from down in Texas. He looks like Texas, too, and it's a shame he can't wear a ten-gallon hat with his uniform.

He doesn't smoke or drink, but how he can cuss! He says alcohol doesn't mix with nitroglycerin, and using nitroglycerin is his normal business. For by vocation and hobby Tex is an oil-well fire fighter. He says there are only three men in America doing his kind of fire-fighting. And he says he's the best-looking one of the three.

Tex loves fires more than anything on earth. He almost goes crazy thinking of all the wonderful fires here in London, and him way down in southern England drilling recruits. But Britain is beginning to wake up to Tex. He has a technical education and a lifetime of experience that are wasted on the drill ground. So now he is frequently called to London to make speeches and confer with fire fighters.

When he's in the city he pays his own hotel expenses. He makes about thirty appointments a day. When he leaves a message for anybody he signs it with a rubber stamp that he carries in his pocket. He already knows every important name in the city. He goes around in the rough battle dress of a Canadian sergeant, but admirals and generals don't faze him. In fact, I'm sure he must faze them.

You ought to hear Tex talk. He says more words in one hour than any human being I've ever met. He talks all over the place. He hadn't been in my room five minutes before he was running back and forth like a madman, pulling a theoretical fire hose up to a theoretical blaze. When a friend of mine walked in Tex was down on his knees loading my wastebasket with theoretical nitroglycerin to put out a big crater fire in Texas.

He carries with him constantly an immense black briefcase that weighs fifty pounds. He calls it Bradford University. It is a traveling encyclopedia. No matter what subject or name you mention, Tex will dig in there and find some reference to it. He is inseparable from this briefcase. He works with it the way a ventriloquist works with his dummy. Before you know it the floor is covered with his papers and letters. He reassembles them and puts them back in the briefcase, then litters the floor with them again a dozen times during the evening.

Tex closed his big oil-field fire-fighting business in Corpus Christi last summer, stored all his equipment, sent his family to California, went to Canada and joined up. He did it because he was in Germany after the last war and he says Germans are not the people he wants to run the world. Also, he has an itchy foot.

Mrs. Bradford knew the minute war was declared that Tex would get in it sooner or later. So she was resigned to it.

They have three sons — one working in Death Valley, one in college and one in high school.

Tex was born in Australia, of Texas parents. I asked him if that made him American or Australian, and he said: "If your cat went next door to an oyster shop and gave birth to a litter, would they be oysters or kittens?" At any rate Tex is a Texan.

He fought with Pancho Villa in Mexico. He has been on the Panama police force. He was a friend of Jack London in California. He battled Hoover's soldiers the time they burned the Bonus Army out of

Washington, even though he wasn't in the bonus march and didn't believe in it. He has never collected his own World War bonus.

He is a fanatical admirer of President Roosevelt, and donated three months of his time in 1936 to help reelect him. He has been an engineer superintendent at a CCC camp in Shiloh Park, Tennessee. He has followed oil fields on every continent on the globe. He has gone to military school and six or eight universities and taken dozens of correspondence courses, and he wishes he could live 300 years so he could do all the things he wants to.

Tex is rough-fibered and tough-minded, yet he is informed on every subject under the sun. He uses unusual words and uses them easily and correctly. His mind seethes and foams. He can't tell a single thing without telling twenty other things along with it. He gets continents and decades away from the subject, but he always remembers to get back to it. He just has so much to tell he tries to tell everything at once.

Tex is busier than two dozen bird dogs. He is just fighting this war to a standstill. He wrote more than 700 letters to senators and congressmen urging them to hurry with help for Britain. He carries a hundred indexed file cards of the names of people he must see in London.

He is a friend of Major George Fielding Eliot, of Pat Hurley, of Congressman Dick Kleberg, of Frederick Delano, of Dale Carnegie. He admires Lowell Thomas. He loves to make public speeches.

Tex weighs 190, and has a chest like an ox. He lets you hit him with all your might right in the stomach, and it is like hitting a stone wall. He marches fourteen miles a day carrying a seventy-pound pack and comes home ahead of the column, doing a jig. Officers tell me Tex is one of the greatest inspirations the Canadian Army has. He is tough and he is smart. And he is burning for a fight.

Yet Tex is as bald as an owl, he is slightly deaf, he wears glasses to read with, and he is a grandfather.

Germans, arise and flee from this transplanted scourge of the plains!

Maybe you would like to hear something about the other Americans in England. Well, there are approximately 4000 of them. If you would tell that to any individual American who lives here he would be amazed, because the most gregarious one probably doesn't know more than a hundred. Outside of newspapermen, I haven't met a dozen Americans altogether. But 4000 is the Embassy's figure.

They fall into three groups: Those in business or holding jobs. Those of dual nationality who married Englishmen. Those who came here to retire.

Some 1600 of those 4000 want to go home, and have notified the Embassy to that effect. But there is no way for them to get there unless they fly to Lisbon, and you have to have pull to get a seat on the plane to Lisbon. Unless the United States sends another ship to Ireland, these people are here for the duration. Most Americans think it is ridiculous that our government refuses to let them travel home on British ships, because of the danger, yet forces them to stay here amid constant danger.

Of these 4000 Americans, not more than 200 take an active part in American doings. The rest just go their own ways. They are scattered all over England. The retired people mostly live in the country, out of harm's way. So far as I can learn, only one American has been killed by a bomb in England, and only a few have been hurt. The number of those who have been scared green is not available at the moment.

Americans over here have been very active in donating money to British relief. Furthermore, some sixty American businessmen have formed a mobile division to help fight the invasion if it comes. They furnish their own cars, which have been camouflaged and equipped with machine guns, rifles and "Molotov cocktails." They drill, and wear British uniforms, but they will see action only if the invasion comes as far as London. I understand they would like to enlarge the unit but can't find any more interested Americans.

There are many Americans (not counted in those 4000) serving here with Canadian troops, but they are hard to count because most of them claim to be Canadians. Many of them are like the fellow who was asked the other day where he came from and said "Vancouver, Saskatchewan" — which was like saying Seattle, Nebraska.

The busiest American over here, I think, is a fellow named Gilbert Carr. Back home in 1920 he would have been a typical Babbitt. He belongs to every lodge and society you've ever heard of. He has lived in England twelve years, and represents the Sunmaid Raisin Company.

Through an arrangement with the government, Mr. Carr is allowed to keep his staff of thirty-five people at work by handling dried fruits from Greece, Smyrna and Australia. He used to handle 15,000 tons of American raisins a year, but now he handles only about half that amount, and they are not American raisins.

Mr. Carr knows all about bombs. Acting on the theme of dispersal, he packed up most of his clothes and took them to his warehouse, just in case his house should get hit. That night a bomb went clear through the warehouse, blew it apart, set it afire and burned it to the ground. Mr. Carr lost all his raisins, his records and his pants.

The next night a bomb exploded outside his office window and shattered the place, but nobody was in the office at the time. They cleared up the glass and went back to work. At his house, in Croydon, a bomb fell in the back yard next door and broke all his windows, cracked the walls and blew the doors off the garage. He had a man come the next morning to put the doors back on. That night they were blown off again.

Mr. Carr still lives in the house, with the windows boarded up. He gets home about eight at night, and works on his papers till he goes to sleep, stretched out between two chairs. He is downtown at eight in the morning.

He spends two hours a day on the raisin business. The rest of the day he is working for Britain. He is a director of the American Ambulance, secretary of the American Committee for Air-Raid Relief, and a director of the recently opened Eagle Club for Americans serving with the British forces. He is also a governor of the American Club, a director of the American Chamber of Commerce, adjutant of the American Legion post, and just now he is acting head of the Allied Relief Fund in this country.

He has desks all over town, and shoots around from here to there. He is the guy who is always called on to do things. He has a big heart and a good physique. He's not afraid of bombs, but he says he gets bored with them.

So do I. Bored limp sometimes.

3. A VISIT WITH LOW

London,
March, 1941.

It would be hard to say, I suppose, who is the greatest cartoonist in the world today. But a good many people think it is David Low, and I wouldn't be a bit surprised myself if he were.

Low draws for Lord Beaverbrook's London Evening Standard. He draws, at the most, three cartoons a week. Occasionally he gets a dry spell, calls up the office and says he's tired, and drops down to one a week. When he does this, he finds it just as hard to produce one cartoon a week as three. And yet I think this respite from the daily grind must have some bearing on Low's greatness. As he says, nobody in the world can produce a good cartoon every day.

I went to see Low with fear and trembling, since great names affect me that way. But I needn't have. He is pleasant and companionable, and you feel at ease with him.

His cartoons are the most powerful, often the most scalding, that I have ever seen. Low's own philosophy is toward the socialistic, and he is pugnacious and caustic in his thinking. Yet as he sits in front of his fireplace puffing at his pipe, his voice is soft and his manner gentle. He reminds you of a very young "Foxy Grandpa."

Low is fifty. He is neither big nor small. His hair is nearly gone on top. His eyebrows are black and extremely wide. He has a grand little smile.

For many years he put himself in his cartoons now and then, in just a few quick lines down in the corner. It was mostly eyebrows. You wouldn't think it could be anybody. Yet when you see Low, he looks exactly as in those cartoons.

He wore a beard until a few months ago. He finally shaved it off because it made him a marked man. Everybody recognized him, and he couldn't get any peace. He is no recluse, however. He loves to walk, and is out a good deal. He has many friends and goes out often to dinners and entertainments.

Low speaks with the confidence of one who knows he is a master in his field, yet he speaks with the quiet of a professor, and not as a braggart. And he has a nice sense of self-ridicule too, for he says:

"A cartoonist has it over newspapermen who write, because if somebody doesn't like your cartoon you can always say, 'Well, you just don't understand it.'"

Low is a New Zealander. He has always been a cartoonist. He came to England twenty-two years ago, via the United States, and has never been back to New Zealand. He has a sentimental feeling about his homeland, and fears that a return to the old scenes and old friends after all these years would be disillusioning.

He says he has never felt thoroughly settled in London. He feels that an Australian or New Zealander is more at home in America than in England. His last visit to America was in October, 1936. He saw Jack Dempsey and Father Divine and President Roosevelt.

The Lows subscribe to many American magazines, including Life and the New Yorker. Mrs. Low scans the new fashions in the ads. "We can't buy anything," she says, "so the next best thing is to look at the pictures." The only thing they don't like about American magazines these days is that so many of the cartoons are on the war, and they see enough war cartoons at home.

Low drew for Collier's a while last year, but had to work so many weeks ahead that he felt his cartoons lost their punch, so it was dropped.

He has two daughters — Prudence and Rachel — in their late teens. Both are political-minded. In fact, the whole Low family is a very important part of Low's greatness. The family breakfast is literally a conference. The four of them thresh over the world news for cartoon ideas. As Low says, "We digest it, argue it, analyze it, sing it, act it out, and balance it on our noses."

Out of this intellectual jamboree usually comes a cartoon idea. But not always. For like all great men, Low finds his head nothing but clay sometimes. The day of my visit was an example.

"I got up this morning a complete blank," he told me. "Here historical events by the hundred were just crashing about us, and I couldn't get a thing. Didn't have anything by lunchtime either. Finally at two o'clock I got an idea.

"You can always work when you have to. I started at two, and the cartoon was finished by four. But I'm not going to look at Monday's paper."

Low works at home, and the paper sends a messenger out for his cartoon. He has had a tough winter. Because of air raids, the Standard's engravers wouldn't work after dark. So he had to have his cartoon in their hands by shortly after lunch. "That meant getting up at seven, two hours before daylight, and trying to be funny," Low says. "You ought to try that sometime."

People say David Low is the highest-paid cartoonist in the world. He also makes money from books and radio. Yet his tastes are simple. He says, "I actually prefer a nine-penny seat in the cinema, and I really like cheap cigars better than expensive ones. Just happened to be born that way."

But the Low house in North London is charming and comfortable. It has deep furniture, floor lamps, a cozy log fire and books on each side of the mantel. A nice girl in brown maid's dress lets you in and serves tea. It is more like an American home than an English one.

The house is a $1.10 taxi ride from the Strand. Low himself rides the subways. I did too coming back into town, and had to change three times. At one place when I asked directions of a woman subway guard she said, "Change at Leicester Square, dearie, they'll put you right."

The Low house is a rambling two-story brick one, with a big green garden behind. There have been a good many bombs near by. Low's mother and aunt, who lived a few blocks away, had their house blown up a few days after they had felt a premonition and moved out of it. Despite his eminent position. Low serves his regular turn as fire-bomb watcher in his block every Monday night. He has put out many incendiaries.

Low had always worked in a studio some fifteen minutes' walk from his house. The studio had no telephone, no messages were delivered, and he received no callers. But he now works at home, because of the bombs. He has an elaborate backyard shelter, with an expensive pumping system to keep it dry. But he was never satisfied with it, so he finally shored up one room of his house with heavy steel beams and brick. The whole family sleeps in this room when the raids are bad. The house also is full of buckets of sand, buckets of water, and stirrup pumps.

Low seldom goes to the Standard office. His drawing paraphernalia is spread on a long table at one end of his den. He works at an elbow-high drawing table, and draws standing up. On the average, it takes him about six hours to do his cartoon.

He is his own man. His position in British journalism is unique. Beaverbrook gives him a free hand. He does not have to follow policy. It's not unusual for Beaverbrook to see himself cruelly lampooned by his own cartoonist in his own paper.

Low is very busy and gets busier every day. He says he can't stand having any kind of challenge made to him without taking it up. For instance, he always hated to write, and never felt he could write. But some years ago a publisher asked him to write a book. He couldn't bear to have the publisher think he wasn't capable of it. So he wrote one. Now he has four going all at once.

It was the same way about public speaking. He can now make a public address without getting sick at his stomach. In fact, he broadcasts to America every two weeks, and gets a great satisfaction from it. He feels that you can convey a hundred per cent more with your voice than you can through the printed page.

Low is crazy about the movies. Good or bad, he still likes them. He is also a great fellow to try games. He has played practically every game ever invented, from golf to pinochle. But his interest in such things quickly ebbs. Many of his games he has played only once. He used to sit by the hour playing the player-piano in his living room, but now it's never touched.

I am no autograph collector, yet I couldn't bear to return to America without one of Low's cartoons. So I asked the Evening Standard for one of his originals.

The one they gave me would make you dance with gratitude. I don't know why I was so honored. To begin with, it is a gruesomely powerful war cartoon. A few weeks ago the Standard had it on exhibition in a front window. A bomb fell in the street outside, and blew a jagged hole right through the center of this Low masterpiece. How is that for a double-barreled war souvenir?

I took the cartoon with me out to Low's house. He had not known about the bomb incident. When he saw the hole, it was as though I had handed him the Pulitzer Prize. You never saw anybody so delighted. He thumbtacked the cartoon onto his drawing-board, and inscribed it to me. Then he started walking around the room, thinking and chuckling. To Mrs. Low he said, "I want to put something funny on it. Come on, help me be funny."

But before Mrs. Low could be funny he said, "I've got it," and went to the drawing-board and started writing. And this is what he wrote, in the white space right next to the jagged hole:

"Dear Hitler — Thanks for the criticism. Yours, Low."

And he beamed like a child as he rolled it up and handed it to me.

4. READY FOR HITLER

Dover,
March, 1941.

102

All day long I rode around southeastern England, skirting the coast from the mouth of the Thames to Dover. And somehow I got an impression that Germans wouldn't be welcome in these parts.

I never hope to see again in my lifetime so much barbed wire and so many highway obstructions and roadside blockhouses as I saw in this one day.

Right at the moment the military arm is sick of visitors, so I couldn't get a pass to see all the heavy stuff and the hidden stuff and the trick stuff that Britain has evolved to foil the encroaching villain. But just driving around, almost like a tourist, you are constantly in such a maze of soldiers, camouflaged trucks, half-hidden guns, trenches, pillboxes, lookout towers, blocked roads and endlessly stretching barbed wire that when you finally leave it you begin to feel lonesome and unsafe.

The censorship doesn't permit a description of camouflage, but I saw camouflaged things that would make you split with laughing if it weren't so deadly serious.

Many farmhouses stand empty, for they will be in the line of battle if battle comes. Sheep graze in the fields while soldiers occupy the sheep sheds. A farmer's simple thatched home may be a general's headquarters. Every roadside wood doesn't cover a gun, but you don't know which one does and which one doesn't.

The public is barred from this whole area covering the Channel coast and extending for many miles inland. Those who live in the area can move about freely, but nobody can come in from outside without a special pass.

Each town along the coast is so heavily defended in front that it seems to me impossible for the Germans to make a landing in force directly by water. So the next assumption is that they would land men and tanks and guns inland, by air, and then try to push back and capture a port to establish a bridgehead for water-borne troops. Consequently the cities are as well defended behind as in front. For miles, in a great semicircle behind each city, the fortifications are complex. Roads and fields and fencerows are entangled and blocked. Behind them are hundreds of gun posts in natural craters.

Everywhere in the whole area are soldiers. They stand guard at nearly every side road, and at most of the side streets in the towns and villages. You can see them running, drilling and practicing out in the fields. You meet them in long lines marching down the road, in full kit. Maybe they don't look exactly like men from Mars, but they certainly don't resemble Englishmen.

Although the whole country is already solid with obstruction and defense, men are still working constantly on more and more of the same. If they put much more concrete down here I think the whole end of this island will sink into the sea.

Surprisingly, the towns in this area don't seem like ghost towns at all. Only about a third of the people have been evacuated, and new soldiers coming in more than make up for this decrease in population. In Dover, Ramsgate and Deal the streets are filled with people. The pubs and picture shows operate as usual. The shops are well stocked. Nobody seems to be going around casting haunted looks over his shoulder.

It is next summer that the difference will be really apparent. For this is the Atlantic City and Coney Island section of England, where half a million Londoners come on a holiday to stroll and bathe and lounge. They won't come next summer. For one thing, most of the big hotels are evacuated. For another, the great beaches and promenade decks up on the cliffsides are now all tangled with barbed wire and concrete blocks. And the sands where massed thousands used to lie and relax are now bare and blocked off.

All this is reason enough for the crowds not coming next summer. But the best reason is — the government won't let anybody in. Not even the Germans.

Dover, as you know, is the English city that is closest to France. It is subject both to air raids and to shelling from German guns across the Channel.

I suppose most of you picture Dover as a deserted city, a half-wrecked ghost town. It isn't at all. It is quite alive. Thousands of people are living here and going on with their business. In fact, Dover is not as badly damaged — not nearly so — as Coventry or Bristol. The waterfront is pretty well battered, and most of the buildings there have been evacuated. But the rest of the city carries right on.

The Grand Hotel, where all the American newspapermen stayed during the great air-raiding days of September, 1940, has since had one whole end bombed off. This end simply fell away from the rest of the hotel as though a giant hand had cut it off with a knife. If you look way up at the naked standing wall, which used to be an inside wall, you will see one lone white washbowl still screwed to the wall. They say a newspaperman went away hurriedly, leaving his razor lying on the bowl, shortly before the hotel was hit. Presumably the razor is still there, but there's no way to get to it.

The Dover area gets a bunch of shells from the other side about once a week. But even the ones that land right in town do little damage.

Even a newcomer like myself, after a few minutes of practice looking, can go around town and say, "This was a bomb" or "This was a shell." A shell seems to knock down only just what it hits, instead of wrecking everything all around the way the big bombs do. I saw buildings in Dover that had received direct hits by shells yet had lost only a few feet of brick and stone off one corner.

German planes cross the coast so frequently that cities in this area have six or eight siren warnings a day. In fact, these coastal towns have recently put in effect a dual warning system. The regular siren goes when the planes are first caught by the sound detectors. Then, if the planes come directly overhead, a local warning is sounded. This may be a steam whistle or a compressed-air squawker different from the regular siren.

There was a first warning in Ramsgate while we were there, in midafternoon, and I noticed lots of people take to the shelters.

Ramsgate, incidentally, has a public shelter system that is unique. It is a vast network of tunnels in the chalk rock, winding around underneath the city at an average of sixty feet below the surface. The total length of this network is three and a half miles, and it can be entered from twenty-three different points.

In the event of a night-long blitz the entire population of Ramsgate could crowd into these tunnels. They were started the year before the war and took more than two years to build. In places the tunnel is so big you could lay two railroad tracks side by side. In this part the city has built little "apartments." These cubicles are merely wooden frameworks covered with black burlap. They are about six feet high and have no roof, but they do give some privacy.

These apartments are permanent homes for 1700 Ramsgate people. They live down there like prehistoric people in caves. Some of them have been bombed out of their homes; others are people who are just afraid.

I'll tell you something to show you how wide awake this coastal defense area is. A friend from Tunbridge Wells drove me around. We drove all day, and covered 150 miles. Of course we had the necessary passes to enter the area, but we didn't have any special route mapped out for ourselves and had sent no word ahead.

In midafternoon we drove into Ramsgate, a good seventy-five miles from London. We stopped at a busy corner and asked a traffic policeman the way to the Lord Mayor's office. The policeman was a nice-looking, pleas- ant young fellow. He told us the way, then looked in the car and said:

"Is this Mr. Pyle?"

My first impulse was to dismount from the car and bow to the passing throng, on the assumption that my prowess as a literary gentleman was now recognized in the uttermost corners of the earth. But logic stayed this action. No such conclusion was permissible under the cold light of fact.

The truth is simply that the police all over the area were being notified from one city to the next who we were and what we were about.

In cases like this it is soothing to know that your past life is an open book and your bib is clean. I'm glad now I never even stole watermelons as a boy.

5. GOOD-BYE TO ALL THAT

London,
March, 1941.

The time has almost come for me to start home.

I came over here originally for only a month. Somehow that has stretched on into a fourth month, almost without me being aware of it. The truth is, I like it over here. But I don't like any place as well as America, and I guess it's time I was getting out of England anyway. I don't yet say "rahther" nor "bloody," but I do find myself automatically looking in the right direction for traffic. Another month and I would probably be standing for Parliament from Hants.

After three months in Great Britain I still have no fears about Britain's "sticking it." Of course I would like to say that everybody was made of steel, that nobody ever got scared or panicky, and that every single soul was working himself to the bone for the war. But I have run into people who were petrified by bombs. I have one friend who loses several pounds during every bad raid. I have also been in some badly blitzed places where spirits were getting pretty low and people were wondering just how much more they could take. I have found a good many stories of selfishness and of running away by people who could afford to run away.

But none of these is expressive of the national character. What you have read in the daily papers back home about Britain's courage and calmness as a nation is absolutely true. Maybe there is something that would break them, but it hasn't come yet.

Britain as a whole is of one mind. I have never heard any defeatist or appeasement talk. Even on the Clydeside and in Wales I heard very little of "this is a capitalistic war" kind of talk.

It is my feeling that the people are ahead of the government in the national will to win; that much of the government still waits to cast a timid political eye at the tides of opinion and the shades of precedent before acting; and that only a few are of the stripe of Churchill and Beaverbrook, with the capacity for complimenting their people's intelligence by moving boldly.

On the whole I have worked up a feeling, from 2000 miles of travel over Britain, that the war effort is not yet supreme. Thousands and thousands of people want to do something to help but are given no direction, no orders. The organization of the war effort seems to me far from perfect. Talent and time and desire to serve are wasted.

As far as I could gather during my travels, the mass of the British people aren't thinking much about war aims. They haven't any very specific ideas of their own. They hope for a better world somehow, but they are pretty vague about it. The chief thought right now is to get the war finished, and then fix it so Germany can't do this thing again to the next generation.

The most important person in the British government, as far as I am concerned, is a Welsh girl named Gwyn Barker who handles the wants of American newspapermen at the Ministry of Information. She is the most thorough, punctual and altogether satisfactory government representative I've ever dealt with. Furthermore, she is personally delightful. In Welsh her name is spelled "Gwynedd."

It seems to me Americans are wasting their time worrying about what the war will do to the characters of the children. They fall so quickly into a familiarity with the ways of war that it becomes wholly natural to them.

One afternoon in Bristol I called on the Rev. Mr. Murray, vicar of St. Michael's Church. The Murrays have a very robust young son named John, nineteen months old, who paddles around the room and says a few words. A few months ago when he heard a plane, John would go to the door, point up and mumble "Airplane." But now when he hears one he points up and says, "Airplane — boom!"

London is "cleaner" than when I came here. Bomb wreckage, except that of the previous two or three nights, is all pushed back of the sidewalks. Many places have been entirely cleared away and now stand as vacant lots. Every day the great rubble heap on the grass of Hyde Park grows bigger. It now covers acres, and it is only one of many.

The open basement of what was Lewis' great store is now almost clear. A new sidewalk is being laid in front of the hole. Almost no streets are now closed by that strange English sign "Diversion."

Things are growing tighter daily. There will soon be meatless days officially, and in hard fact they are here already. Only a few silk stockings are left on sale. Radio sets are limited from now on. The railroads may soon raise their fares again. The Home Guards must wear their uniforms to work. Conscription of labor is in the balance.

Gas drills are being held in various suburbs. Recent tests showed some masks "out of fit" — gas gets in through the side. Four hundred masks a day are being lost or left on subway trains. The newspapers continually berate the public about not carrying masks, yet not one person in a hundred does it.

Now that the lend-lease bill is law, the British talk more frankly to Americans. "Why shouldn't you give us the stuff?" my barber asks. "You don't ask a man to repay you a shilling when you're both running for your lives."

It is the belief of most Americans I know over here that America is headed rapidly toward war. Their feeling seems about fifty-fifty for and against the idea.

More and more Americans are rolling in — here to study this, and study that.

Books about the war are coming out by the dozen, but no masterpiece seems to have been written yet.

New stage plays are opening all the time. "Gone With the Wind" is running into its second year, and you have to get seats ahead of time. Leslie Howard is making a film. Lawrence Olivier has passed his R.A.F. medical examination.

The air war is picking up. There is a lot of sudden dying in London every night. It is hit-and-skip dying. It is death dealt by mystic lottery. A lone bomber three miles above in the dark lets one loose. That bomb will hit some small spot in a big area thirty miles across, it will pick out some doomed handful from among London's eight million people. Until it hits, nobody knows.

Ten may die tonight out of the eight million. What marked those ten to be drawn in the lottery instead of us? What fate drew a bomb to their special hundred square feet? My room is the same size as theirs, why didn't it come here? There is no answer. That's why you get so you don't pay any attention.

There is no feeling of stringency or acuteness in daily life. People seem to live even more laxly than when I first came here. They know something is bound to come — but I am certain the public is not worrying about it.

The war is not dramatic to the British people. They go from day to day and take care of whatever happens. There is no fury, no frenzy, no great hatred, no general fear, no fanaticism. Faces look the same as in peacetime. There is no urgency in the British demeanor. In three months I have not met an Englishman to whom it has ever occurred that Britain might lose the war.

Now it is time to go. It is not easy to leave. There is something about leaving England in wartime that you cannot bear. I have been all around to say my good-byes, and I have told them all that it was not good-bye forever, that I would be back.

Spring comes early in England, and it is a lovely thing. Already the days are soft and gentle. It is wonderful to be alive when warmth and freshness spreads over the land. All through England people are looking forward to the real, blooming fulness of spring. For many of them, it will never happen. I could not bear to think that for me there might never, never be another spring.

106

EPILOGUE

Albuquerque, N. M.

The long trip home is done. The wars are far distant, and over the desert there hangs an infinity of space and time that seems put here to prohibit any contemplation of giant struggles far away.

It is so quiet out here just at dawn. I don't know what, but something awakens us — the silence or the gentleness — something awakens us just at daybreak. And we get up, and watch the light come softly over the bare Sandias to the east, and it is a perfect hour. The little birds hop from the sage-filled mesa at daylight, and they come over into our yard and they peck in the fresh earth, and waddle around and sing and have a wonderful time.

The friendly hot sun makes its arc across the peaceful sky, and evening is here. We have a window which looks to the west, and every evening I sit there and watch. Just as the sun touches the horizon its gold radiates upward onto the hanging clouds above, and the unearthly long line of the mesa rim turns into a silhouette and the old volcano peaks stand silently black in their filament of fire, and all out and on beyond, everywhere, is the gentle rolling vastness of the desert. What you see then from our west window is something completely enthralling, something that is big, and finer than any words.

All this is here for us to relish, so lovely and beautiful and serene. But when we sit in our west window at sundown it is past midnight in London, and the guns are going and the bombers are raising hell and my friends of yesterday are tense and full of a distracting excitement — peering, listening, alert to death and the sounds of death.

Out here, so remote from turmoil, the ghostly rustle of a falling bomb can surely be only something you dreamed once in a nightmare. There can be no truth in it. And yet you know. Day and night, always in your heart, you are still in London. You have never really left. For when you have shared even a little in the mighty experience of a compassionless destruction, you have taken your partnership in something that is eternal. And amidst it or far away, it is never out of your mind.

Made in the USA
Monee, IL
26 April 2021